PROSPECT HIGH: BROOKLYN

by
Daniel Robert Sullivan

Chanique Peart

Paul Tanis

Aaliyah Stewart

Deshaye Tingling

Amanda Rodriguez

Isaiah Latimer

Jaylin Acosta

Shannon Deep

Rebecca Powell

Brandy Brown

Azaria Guthrie

Rachel Friedman

Original Cover Design by Darren Melchiorre

LICENSING & PRODUCTION INQUIRIES
Uproar Theatrics, LLC.
hello@uproartheatrics.com I www.UproarTheatrics.com

Prospect High: Brooklyn had its first workshop and reading at Roundabout Theatre Company in April 2014.

Original Workshop Cast

ANDREA: Jeanette Dilone
DEVIN: Amara James Aja
ANNY: Khalid Rivera
BRIA: Ivy Haralson
MR. CHARLES: Daniel Robert Sullivan

Original Direction by: Shelley Butler
Dramaturg: Shannon Deep
Stage Manager: Julia Borowski

Further development took place under the direction of Christopher V. Edwards at the Nevada Conservatory Theatre, in association with the University of Nevada-Las Vegas, in September 2015.

During the 2015-16 academic year, Prospect High: Brooklyn became the first play in history to have a Rolling World Premier in high schools. The following bold and inclusive theatre departments were chosen to present:

Broad Ripple Magnet High School for the Arts and Humanities, Indianapolis
Ridgeway High School, Memphis
Trinity Academy for the Performing Arts, Providence
Corcoran High School, Syracuse
Leon High School, Tallahassee
Academy at Palumbo, Philadelphia
Boston Arts Academy, Boston
Central High School, Bridgeport
Capital Area School for the Arts, Harrisburg
Milwaukee High School of the Arts, Milwaukee
Pioneer High School, Ann Arbor
Youth Performing Arts High School, Louisville
Southwest High School, Minneapolis
Harding Fine Arts Academy, Oklahoma City
Lincoln High School, San Jose
Niles West High School, Chicago
Grand Prairie Fine Arts Academy, Dallas
Philadelphia School for Creative and Performing Arts, Philadelphia
Nassau BOCES Long Island High School for the Arts, Long Island
McCallum Fine Arts Academy, Austin
San Diego School of Creative and Performing Arts, San Diego
Baltimore School for the Arts, Baltimore
Repertory Company High School for Theatre Arts, New York City

Acknowledgments:

Prospect High: Brooklyn was devised by Daniel Robert Sullivan in response to his perception of a current dearth of issue-driven, easily-producible, flexible-cast plays for teenage actors to perform. Co-writers are New York City high school students Chanique Peart, Paul Stoll, Aaliyah Stewart, Deshaye Tingling, Isaiah Latimer, Amanda Rodriguez, Jaylin Acosta, Brandy Brown, and Azaria Guthrie, who participated in six months of workshops led by Daniel Robert Sullivan in Roundabout Theatre Company's Education Department. The dialogue in the play comes directly from their real conversations and in many cases is preserved verbatim. Without their honesty, openness, and willingness to share, we would never have such a clear picture of what some teenagers are thinking about here in New York. Grateful acknowledgment must also be given for the significant improvements offered by Shelley Butler and Shannon Deep, and the insight granted by undergraduate actors and directors at UNLV.

Financial and creative support provided by Roundabout Theatre Company's Education Department, Theatre Communications Group, and the Fox Foundation.

Daniel Robert Sullivan and Roundabout Theatre Company are participants in the Fox Foundation Resident Actor Fellowships, funded by the William & Eva Fox Foundation and administered by Theatre Communications Group.

"When we had our first table read, my students' initial reaction was, 'This play is too real; it's like they know us.' There was an immediate connection to the play, not only because these characters are three-dimensional representations of urban students, but because we have recently suffered a wave of teenage violence in Bridgeport. We see this play as a means to engage our community in a difficult conversation about violence. This play gives voice to students who often have no voice in our society. We couldn't be more proud to be presenting such a timely, mature, and explosive new play." Shaun Mitchell, Central High School, Bridgeport

"This is a play that lots of people need to see." Rebecca Marten, Milwaukee High School of the Arts

"This is a dynamic, gritty new play devised with authentic student voices grappling with challenges of connection, isolation, sexual identity, friendship, stress, and violence. Often crafted as sequences of two-hander scenes, the play is terrific for performance ensembles large and small, as well as scene study classes. This urban tale addresses contemporary teen issues without apology - and is told by characters that are funny, moving, and at times, scary. I believe this play is a major new voice for TYA." James. T. Jack, George Street Playhouse

"That was some deep shit." Audience member, Trinity Academy for the Performing Arts, Providence

"Although this play is about high school students, it is by no means a 'high school' play. Prospect High: Brooklyn genuinely reflects urban student's lives, the ways they speak and the real life issues they face, without creating stereotypes. My students immediately connected with the words and the characters, many finding their lives written on the page. Because of this, they are inspired to perform to try to change minds, perceptions, and stigma about who the urban student is." Rebecca Marten, Milwaukee High School of the Arts

"This is the first time in 14 years our school has moved on to the state finals. Prospect High brought us there." Bryan Mitchell, Leon High School, Tallahassee

"They hit some people pretty hard last night; tears on faces as they walked out of the theatre." Tonya Wilkison, Broad Ripple High School, Indianapolis

"We have a culturally diverse cast of kids who were drawn to the project because of the real life issues presented in the play. Our small black box venue allows the audience to see up close and personal the struggles these young characters face on a daily basis. In the early days of our rehearsals, the kids shared memories of witnessing or being a part of bullying and violence. The kids used these memories as a foundation from which to build their characters." Lisa Weitzman, Capital Area School for the Arts Charter School, Harrisburg

"That butterfly scene is the most truthful and profound way the issue of cutting has ever been talked about." Student, Long Island High School for the Arts, Nassau County

"This play is such an authentic representation of its characters and setting. It speaks to the diversity of the high school experience while portraying a specific community." Aliza Greenberg, The Learning Spring School, New York

"It was unbelievable. I forgot I was watching actors. That script is amazing and so well written. Each character was developed so magnificently that it was tough to find a favorite. These messages need to be seen!" Friedrika Robinson, parent, Trinity Academy for the Performing Arts, Providence

"I think what Prospect High so importantly achieves is that it humanizes violence. We are rooting for Devin, empathizing with him, and can see that deep down, his violence is the expression of incredibly deep pain and longing and confusion. In a society that is reflexively punitive and that demonizes young black men, I think this is profoundly valuable." Daniel Cantor, University of Michigan

"From the first table read, my students have been connected to the characters of Prospect High: Brooklyn. The issues faced by teenagers are universal no matter where they live. They are keenly aware that violence is a threat to their population on a daily basis with steady reminders from our 'run, hide, and defend' drills." Chuck Manthe, Lincoln High School, San Jose

"It is very difficult to find large-cast pieces for student actors, and this play has presented the opportunity for my students to work with a subject matter that is relevant and timely to them. There is not an issue in the play that has not affected a member of the cast in a direct way." Dr. Marlene Goebig, Philadelphia School for Creative and Performing Arts

"While the play investigates a wide swath of issues that concern young people, at its core it is a story about how our failures to communicate and empathize, to hear each other - across divides of age, race, gender, and circumstance - can have dire consequences. That those failures, combined with the stresses of poverty, and of societal and institutional indifference, engender a kind of desperation, which in turn can result in violence. That is, Prospect High investigates the multiple root causes that might make a young person susceptible to violence. The play doesn't pretend to offer an answer to the systemic problems of our culture except to say that the first step is, and must be, listening." Daniel Cantor, University of Michigan

"This play has reached out to the student demographic here at Leon in powerful ways. It's a play for the time. There are very few plays written for high school students; most are too old, too young, or out of date. The kids love the opportunity to play characters closer to their age and in situations they can relate to." Bryan Mitchell, Leon High School, Tallahassee

"This is a one-of-a-kind project. Hats off to you; you've achieved precisely what you aimed to achieve." Daniel Cantor, University of Michigan

"Even though some of the stuff was hard to hear, it needed to be heard." Audience member, Lincoln High School, San Jose

WHO

Andrea: freshman, female, spunky
Devin: sophomore, male, volatile
Anny: junior, transgender, joyous
Bria: senior, female, forceful
Mr. Charles: teacher, male, placid

All characters may be any race/ethnicity, but please attempt to represent actual demographics when possible. Medium-cast version also introduces us to Mr. Curran, Justice, Bridgett, Daria, Mr. D, Mr. Nichols, and Makala. Large-cast version includes the aforementioned, plus Lewis, Danielle, Kiarra, Rachel, Jessica, and Milan.

WHAT
Devised from real events and real people.

WHERE
Brooklyn, NY
Prospect High School

WHEN
October
Tuesday
2:47 PM

HOW
The play may be performed with five, twelve, or eighteen actors. The small-cast version is printed here, with notes for medium and large-cast adjustments. Other variations also permitted. Curse word substitution allowed. Music encouraged.

Alternate word substitutions appear in brackets. A slash indicates a character should begin speaking at this point in the previous character's line. Ensemble may be added to scenes and transitions at director's discretion.

A NOTE ON CASTING:

The co-creators of this play believe quite strongly that the characters may be cast with actors of any race/ethnicity in any role, but encourage you to represent actual demographics when possible. At the time of publication, the student population in the Brooklyn neighborhood in which this fictional high school would probably be located is 70% Black, 15% Hispanic, 9% White, and 2% Asian. Broadening to all of New York City's public school population, the demographics are 41% Hispanic, 26% Black, 16% Asian, and 15% White.

The teacher roles were created by a white male, though it is reasonable and acceptable to cast a female in these roles. If using a female actor, please change "Mike Palmer" in the PROLOGUE to "Marisa Palmer," "the two Michaels" in GOOD ADVICE to "the two Kellys," "Adam Charles" in CALL HOME to "Shawn Charles," and adjust line to read: "It's *Ms.* Shawn Charles. It's ok; I get that a lot." Any race/ethnicity is also possible, though the subtleties of privilege are more realistically addressed when casting a white male. Also note that the teacher roles are most effective when not played for laughs. His/her opinions are offered in absolute sincerity and reactions remain mostly placid.

Anny was created with the intention that she is a transgender girl. She is likely passing, and this probably is a factor in her generally positive experience at school. This role can be cast with a non-passing male, but the experience may become less authentic; it is our belief that a passing individual has an easier time in this environment. It is also possible, though also less authentic, to cast a transgender boy in the role. If doing so, please make the following adjustments: change the character name to ANDY, change the line in FRESHMAN/SENIOR from "booty-bouncing" to "bouncing around," reverse the pronouns in FRESHMAN/ SENIOR and CALL HOME, and change the mistake in CALL HOME from "Anny-Antonio" to "Anny-Andy."

Please use the alternate EXPRESS HERSELF scene found at the back of the play.

PROLOGUE

*At rise, we see a burst of text: "Inspired by
actual events." We see news anchors.
Character assignments following each line are
suggestions only, and may be adjusted.*

Good evening. Nightly News starts tonight with a teenage
victim who was held captive, beaten, and maimed. And
what's more, the suspects are teenagers themselves. The
Night Team's Mike Palmer is live tonight with details. Mike?
(ANDREA)

Two teenagers from Prospect High School are accused in the
case of a young man who was lured into a secluded area of
the school and tortured. The suspects were discovered by a
teacher shortly after 4:00 today while beginning to carve into
the victim's forehead with a box cutter. (MR. CHARLES)

Two teens are facing kidnapping and assault charges after
police say they tortured one of their classmates, attacking
him with a hammer and other tools while keeping him bound
in a stairwell. (BRIA)

We see a panel of news commentators.

Ok, so a student bringing a gun to school isn't unheard of. It
happened at MLK, at Kennedy. I think it was four or five
times in New York last year. But torture? That's a new / one.
(DEVIN)

Thugs! You're talking about a couple of / thugs! (ANDREA)

C'mon, you can't say / that! (MR. CHARLES)

What is happening to our schools? (ANDREA)

1

Well, this isn't the norm! You've got to remember that. This isn't happening / every day. (MR. CHARLES)

They're probably alllll on drugs! (ANDREA)

The question, really, is what do we need to do to prevent this kind of thing from / happening at all? (ANNY)

Fix the achievement gap! You run these numbers: different populations of kids are not learning at the same / rate! (BRIA)

Because they're all choosing violence! (ANDREA)

Two voices respond together.

No! (DEVIN & MR. CHARLES)

Not all of them! Not all of them are choosing / violence. (DEVIN)

I'd say the main issue is poverty. We can agree on that, I / think. (ANNY)

But there's no work ethic! Do they get a summer break in *China*?! No, they do / not! (ANDREA)

Yes, they do. They do get a summer break in / China. (DEVIN)

A chaotic school does not mean a violent school! (ANNY)

But actual *torture*? / C'mon! (DEVIN)

High stakes testing, Common Core; it's too much / pressure! (BRIA)

I think maybe it is about a lack of / connection. (MR. CHARLES)

They took *prayer* out of our schools, they took God out of our schools, and our schools took a trip to hell! (ANDREA)

How did you get on this panel? (ANNY)

Politicians are not gonna solve this from - (BRIA)

> *Two voices respond together.*

the top down! (BRIA & ANNY)

That's right! (ANNY)

It's not about changing policies. It's not about changing / laws. (DEVIN)

And where are the parents?! (BRIA)

Then what do you do? You want to stop the violence - what do you do? Specifically. (MR. CHARLES)

Well, I don't have an answer, but that's what we're trying to figure out, isn't it? How to stop this violence – that's what we're trying to figure out. (DEVIN)

> *We hear sounds signifying the end of a school day.*

FRESHMAN/SENIOR

Note: In medium and large cast versions, this scene remains
BRIA and ANDREA, with DEVIN.

> *Outside the principal's office. Perhaps a clock
> shows 2:47 and continues to run in real time
> throughout the play. ANDREA works feverishly
> on some schoolwork. Although both are
> extremely confident, BRIA is much brassier
> about it all. We hear BRIA's voice offstage
> overpowering a male voice, "Baby. C'mon,
> now." BRIA is very, very loud.*

                    BRIA
No, Isaac, get off! Why are you talking to me?! Get off! I
won't hesitate to slap you, Isaac. I will not hesitate to slap
you!

> *BRIA enters.*

I can't wait to leave this place! These people are mad crazy!

                    ANDREA
I know.

> *BRIA tries to see if the principal is available, but
> his door is very closed.*

                    BRIA
Shut up, what do you know?

                    ANDREA
Ok.

BRIA

Isaac. I cannot *handle* that kid! That boy is lucky I didn't take him down, he's a little punk. Who are you?

ANDREA

Andrea.

BRIA

You're a freshman.

ANDREA

Yup.

BRIA

I hate you guys. I mean, no offense, but y'all crazy.

ANDREA

Ok.

BRIA

I'm so done with this shit!

ANDREA

You seem like it.

BRIA

You being sarcastic with me?!

ANDREA

No. You just seem like you are so done with this shit.

BRIA

Yeah, I gotta get out! Prospect, I'm done with you!

ANDREA

Hey, / keep it -

BRIA

I'm sick! This new principal - he's saying he's getting us
ready for college. Well, I don't need all this preparedness!
I'm taking care of it myself! I've been in school like eight
hours a day since freshman year. I'm a senior! I want a break
- you know what I'm saying?

ANDREA

You're a senior. You want a break.

RIA

Yeah, I do. 2:50. Almost eight hours today!

ANDREA

That's life. No breaks.

ANDREA references her schoolwork.

BRIA

Oh, that's life, huh?! How old are you?

BRIA yells into the office door.

Yo, we need a break!

ANDREA

Hey -

Confrontational.

BRIA

What?

ANDREA

Just - keep it down. He'll freak out, trust me.

BRIA

He's *already* freaking out! That "silent lunch." 1800 kids here - he wants us to sit in a lunch room forty-five minutes and not talk? Naw. "If you guys don't quiet down, you get silent lunch. For the rest of your high school!"

ANDREA

When did he say that?

BRIA

Are you serious? Today. Today at lunch! Anny dancing up on the table -

ANDREA

Dancing? She was full on twerking.

BRIA

Ok, yeah, that shit was funny.

ANDREA

Booty-bouncing and busts out a ceiling tile.

BRIA

Yo, he's crazy!

ANDREA

She's crazy. She likes to be called "she" -

Confrontational.

BRIA

I know that. Anny's my friend.

ANDREA

Mine, too.

BRIA

Well, good for you. How do you know him - her? She's a junior.

ANDREA

Grew up two buildings down. We're like best friends since middle school.

BRIA

She's got it going on. You could learn from that one, you know what I'm saying?

ANDREA

You're saying she's got it going on and I could learn / from that one.

BRIA

Yooo, you seriously gotta check that.

ANDREA

Sorry - what are you waiting on?

BRIA

Him! New principal. What's his name?

ANDREA

Feliciano. Probably gonna be a while.

BRIA

Well, *apparently* he's the only one that can sign off on me dropping AP English.

ANDREA

Why you doing that?

BRIA

'Cause I got honor roll every semester!

ANDREA

So, why are / you -

BRIA

Every one!

ANDREA

Yeah, so / why -

BRIA

And this one class is bringing me down! I never even wanted to take it! Like I had my mind *set*. Over the summer, "Yes, I'm a senior. I'm not gonna take *one* more AP class." Come September: AP English, AP Bio - I was like, "Stop. I did *not* sign up for this shit."

ANDREA

You finished your other credits.

BRIA

Yes! They may as well give me my diploma right now! I can get into City College *today*. So, why do I have to do more, you know what I'm saying?

ANDREA

You're saying why do you / have -

BRIA

Yooo!

ANDREA

College credit.

BRIA

What?

ANDREA

You do the AP class for college credit.

BRIA

No, that class is getting in the *way* of my college.

ANDREA

Only if you let it, you know what I'm saying?

BRIA

Ooo. What are you, some kinda - ?

ANDREA

Yes. Yes, I am.

RIA

Yo, you do not *know*! Last year was beautiful for seniors. Started late, got out early. Now we got extra classes; he's changing *everything*!

ANDREA

He doesn't like things easy.

BRIA

That's what I'm saying!

ANDREA

I'm supposed to check in with him every day.

BRIA

Check in for what?

ANDREA

Just this end of day thing.

BRIA

Never heard of *that* before. Shit, that's crazy!

ANDREA

"Hello. I have survived. Check."

BRIA

See, he doesn't know what he's doing.

ANDREA

No, it's not / that he -

BRIA

He's controlling.

ANDREA

He says they brought him here 'cause this place *has* no control. He's right; lot of people fight here.

BRIA

Naw, they just talk.

ANDREA

It's violent.

BRIA

I have seen violent. This ain't [isn't] it.

ANDREA

But people here -

BRIA

Don't. I know what violent looks like. But nine out of ten - kids *here* are not about that life.

ANDREA

Lot of police around this school.

                            BRIA
Facts.

                          ANDREA
So kids fight in the bodegas [park], on the bus.

                            BRIA
They're not fighting! Mostly girls just screaming at each
other; that's not violent! You seen the video of that one on
the nine bus?

                          ANDREA
Yeah, she got like Facebook famous.

                            BRIA
But she was just *yelling*. "Real Red Rachel."

                          ANDREA
Rachel, yeah. That video kinda got viral.

                            BRIA
She should have put that up on World Star.

                          ANDREA
I know! People want to get famous on YouTube for - you
know - talent? Forget that, there's World Star. You get
famous for pulling out some girl's weave!

                            BRIA
Get famous for being on your knees, too.

                          ANDREA
Yes!

                        TOGETHER
World Star Candy!

Laughter, then BRIA is impatient again.

BRIA
Yo, what is he *doing* in there?

ANDREA
I don't know; he's always locked in. You can go first.

BRIA
Your "check-in" gonna take that long?

ANDREA
No. I just - you can just go first. If you want.

BRIA
Good. I just have to drop this class.

ANDREA
Well, you don't *have* to.

BRIA
Why do you *talk* like that?! You freshmen will always be forever disrespectful.

ANDREA
And you seniors will / always -

BRIA
You really want to say that?

ANDREA
No, I do not.

BRIA
This is real life; / you gotta watch it.

ANDREA

This is not real life! This is high school; this is fake life.

BRIA

You'll see.

ANDREA

I do see! You can be whoever you want here - look at Anny - it's not a problem. But everybody acts all fake! Teenagers are horrible.

BRIA

Naw, most of these kids are just dumb. And these teachers -

ANDREA

Teachers aren't the problem.

BRIA

They hate us! You don't even / know.

ANDREA

They just can't relate / to us.

BRIA

They hate their jobs and they take it out on us!

ANDREA

You've gotta choose to calm down.

BRIA

I've gotta choose not to slap your face right now, that's what I've gotta choose.

ANDREA

I talk too much.

BRIA

Yeah, we agree.

ANDREA

Sucky week. You know Devin?

BRIA

Yeah, I know Devin. How do you know him?

ANDREA

We've been together since this summer.

BRIA

Seriously?! That's my cousin!

ANDREA

Devin is your cousin?

BRIA

Yeah!

ANDREA

No way.

BRIA

For real! You're his girlfriend?!

ANDREA

Yeah.

BRIA

Shoot. Where *is* he?

ANDREA

He's around. Just staying home a lot.

BRIA

Devin's a good guy. Got issues, though.

ANDREA

I know. So do I.

BRIA

Alllll y'all freshmen have issues.

ANDREA

Devin's not a freshman.

BRIA

I know that.

ANDREA whips out her phone.

ANDREA

You follow his Instagram?

BRIA

Don't let them see that.

ANDREA

I know. You follow him?

BRIA

No.

ANDREA

He posts this psycho picture today:

We see and hear DEVIN as the girls read.

DEVIN
"Here's a thought: you harass somebody and they don't fight back? Maybe you'd better start getting scared of their breaking point."

BRIA
That about you?

ANDREA
No!

BRIA
It's like a warning.

ANDREA
No, it's attention-seeking behavior.

BRIA
Attention what?

ANDREA
Classic attention-seeking behavior. I hate it.

BRIA is starting to be amused by this little freshman.

BRIA
Ok. Ok, I got you.

ANDREA
It used to be all nice. Just like a million pictures of us:

DEVIN
"Andrea knows me inside; you all just see what I'm putting out front."

ANDREA

A couple weeks ago:

DEVIN

"She's hot, she's funny, and she's too smart for me. I'm
lucky this girl sticks around."

BRIA

You're lucky, too.

ANDREA

I know that! I know. Last month:

DEVIN

"Love that girl."

BRIA

Love?

ANDREA

That's what he's putting out there, yeah. But *fake*! Oh my
god, why doesn't he act like that in real life instead of just
online?

BRIA

Still nice. That's better than most girls get.

ANDREA

Yeah, I guess.

Playful now.

BRIA

Every school's got their Romeo and Juliet.

ANDREA

Please, I am *not* Juliet; she is dumbest girl ever. Sorry, I'm not gonna go killing myself over any guy.

BRIA

Romeo put himself on the line for her.

ANDREA

Yeah, but then he was so dumb! He couldn't tell if his girlfriend was asleep or dead?! I'm sorry; you wanna be with someone, you've gotta at least be able to know whether they're asleep or dead.

BRIA

Yeah, ok!

Perhaps pensive.

ANDREA

You've gotta be able to look at them and know what's going on.

BRIA

We talking about my cousin now?

ANDREA

Maybe.

BRIA

You know, it's hard to tell if shit's serious or not.

ANDREA

Not really, / all you have -

BRIA

Ok, Devin *saved* me from some serious shit one time. He's good to have around.

ANDREA

I know that, / but -

BRIA

Hey, I don't know where you're from, but here sometimes
you need a little protection. Shit around here might look bad
all the time, but you gotta be able to tell the difference
between bad and *dangerous*. And he can. Better than me, I
guess. Devin put himself on the line for me; I owe him, big
time.

ANDREA

I think he's gonna fight Isaac.

BRIA

Good, Isaac's an ass. You gotta *learn* about Isaac.

ANDREA

I know about him.

BRIA

No. Let me give you this: don't ever be alone near that punk.

ANDREA

Ok.

BRIA

Just don't.

ANDREA

Ok. He's making Devin all crazy.

BRIA

Devin's always been crazy.

ANDREA

Yeah?

BRIA

When he's pushed, yeah.

ANDREA

Well he's getting pushed.

BRIA

He's gotta push back.

ANDREA

No.

BRIA

He knows; he's gotta push back or he's gonna get stepped
on.

ANDREA

No, 'cause then he goes off on people, and he's acting just
like them!

BRIA

Devin's never gonna be like Isaac.

ANDREA

He's getting to be.

BRIA

Nobody here's as bad as Isaac. / Nobody.

ANDREA

Devin's getting to be. You haven't even seen him lately.

BRIA

I've known him forever.

ANDREA

Something's different, / though.

BRIA

I know my cousin!

ANDREA

I know him, too! I know / him, too!

BRIA

Woah - woah! You're not gonna survive here you keep talking to people like this.

ANDREA

Sorry, it's just - Anny showing off, Rachel fighting, Devin freaking out; it feels fake!

BRIA

It's real life, / girl.

ANDREA

And sorry, but you, too.

BRIA

Me what?

ANDREA

Why are you standing here? Sorry, I just don't get it; why are you trying to drop a class that gets you college credit just 'cause of the teacher?

BRIA

I can't have an F!

ANDREA

So work it back up!

                    BRIA
And that teacher -

                    ANDREA
Failing you, I know.

                    BRIA
You think you know / a lot.

                    ANDREA
Maybe stop caring so much about it; you're smart enough to
work it back up. One grade? Who cares?

                    BRIA
Who are *you* / to tell - ?

                    ANDREA
I'm not! I'm no one! And I'm a freshman, so you won't
listen to me anyway.

                    BRIA
You talk straight, I'll give you that. But that's no way to win
friends.

                    ANDREA
I know - gotta be fake to win friends. Maybe that's why I
only have Anny.

                    BRIA
And Devin.

                    ANDREA
Sometimes Devin.

                    BRIA
I'm not sure what to say to you, freshman.

ANDREA

Hasn't stopped you for the last ten minutes.

BRIA

Ohhhhh!

ANDREA

I'm kidding - don't hurt me. *I don't know what I'm doing!* I can't handle this place; it's insane.

BRIA

Facts.

Imitating ANNY.

ANDREA

"Preach!"

A moment. A smile.

BRIA

This guy's still not coming out!

ANDREA

Feliciano.

BRIA

Yeah, Mister Feliciano. Ugh.

BRIA begins to exit.

ANDREA

You leaving?

BRIA

Maybe. Yeah.

ANDREA

What about dropping AP English?

BRIA

It's fine, whatever.

And maybe ANDREA shows a hint of pride.

ANDREA

Wait - wait! Please. You're not gonna drop it?

BRIA

No - *I don't care*! That's what you want to hear, right?!
Gonna make things harder, but I'll figure it out.

ANDREA

I'm gonna go, too.

BRIA

Thought he told you to do the check-in thing?

ANDREA

He tells me a lot of things.

BRIA

I'm Bria, by the way.

ANDREA

I know. Hi, Bria.

BRIA

What did you say your name was?

ANDREA

Andrea. Andrea Feliciano.

Realization. A smile.

> BRIA

Feliciano?

> ANDREA

Yeah.

> BRIA

Like - ?

> ANDREA

Yeah.

> BRIA

Oh, you're a piece of work.

> ANDREA

I like to think so.

BRIA exits with purpose, ANDREA behind her.

GOOD ADVICE

Note: In medium and large cast versions, this scene is MR.
CURRAN and DEVIN.

> *In a classroom. DEVIN clutches a backpack*
> *throughout. In the large-cast version of the play,*
> *DEVIN is the only character to appear in*
> *multiple full scenes.*

MR. CHARLES

Five days out, I think. Five days out in the past two weeks.

DEVIN

I guess.

MR. CHARLES

So, I mean, c'mon. You gotta show up or you get no credit.
That's the rules. I mean, do what you want, but even a D is
better than no credit.

DEVIN

Yeah.

MR. CHARLES

Child Services calls home after seventeen days. You close to
seventeen days yet?

DEVIN

Past it.

MR. CHARLES

Devin, it's October.

DEVIN

Yeah.

MR. CHARLES
Ok, so that's the rules, too. They'll contact your mother.

DEVIN
Please don't let them do that.

MR. CHARLES
I've got no control over that, Devin! Now, what was up
today?

DEVIN
That whole thing was not my fault.

MR. CHARLES
Looked like your fault.

DEVIN
Isaac does that shit all the time.

MR. CHARLES
Watch your language, please.

DEVIN
All the time.

MR. CHARLES
So, you're saying it's Isaac's fault?

DEVIN
I don't know. Calling me a faggot.

MR. CHARLES
Language.

DEVIN
Exactly. He uses shitty language.

MR. CHARLES

Devin! Somebody is to blame here. You're missing half of
my classes, and when you're there, you and Isaac disrupt the
whole room. Rules say I don't suspend you for cutting, but I
have to suspend you for one more disruption. Just so you
know.

DEVIN

The guy is always messing with people! You heard about
him and Bria?

MR. CHARLES

This is not about Bria -

DEVIN

He's bad news, Mr. Charles. You don't even know. He's *still*
got his hands all over her.

MR. CHARLES

And you're saying - he's got his hands all over you?

DEVIN

No!

MR. CHARLES

Well then, what?

DEVIN

Never / mind.

MR. CHARLES

Devin, I am not understanding you!

DEVIN

Never / mind!

MR. CHARLES
What are you saying?!

DEVIN
I'm saying he's frickin' killing me!

MR. CHARLES
"Killing you."

DEVIN
Freshman year same thing, but not anymore. Can I go?

MR. CHARLES
Hold up - I got somewhere to be, too. So, that's *figuratively* "killing you?"

DEVIN
Something like that. Whatever – I'm taking care of it.

MR. CHARLES
Well, taking care of it, good. But it's a question of how, Devin. How?

DEVIN
Don't worry about it.

MR. CHARLES
I'm not really worrying about it. Just need to solve the problem.

DEVIN
I'm solving it.

MR. CHARLES
I know you think you are, but maybe you've actually got to sit down with / somebody -

DEVIN
I'm sitting down! I'm sitting here!

MR. CHARLES
You talked to Mr. Feliciano?

DEVIN
No.

MR. CHARLES
Well.

DEVIN
I can't talk to him about this.

MR. CHARLES
Why not?

DEVIN
Me and Andrea are going out.

MR. CHARLES
Andrea?

DEVIN
His daughter.

MR. CHARLES
Oh. Wow. You talk to her about this?

DEVIN
No.

MR. CHARLES
Well, why not?

                    DEVIN
Mr. Charles, / I can't -

                    MR. CHARLES
Not the principal, not your girlfriend -

                    DEVIN
They're not gonna -

                    MR. CHARLES
You don't talk to anybody?

                    DEVIN
I'm talking to you!

                    MR. CHARLES
Oh! Ok. Then I guess I gotta dig in.

                    DEVIN
You don't have to -

                    MR. CHARLES
Nope! Nope, it's fine. Devin, I actually know what this feels
like.

                    DEVIN
No, you don't.

                    MR. CHARLES
Yup, I do. I mean, do what you want to do, but I'll just say
you *can* get through it.

                    DEVIN
I know.

                    MR. CHARLES
Ok!

DEVIN

Can I go?

MR. CHARLES

Almost. For me it was these two guys, the two Michaels.
They were awful to me in the eighth grade. Bullies! But I
hate that word 'cause it's so overused these days, / right?

DEVIN

Mr. Charles, it's not bullying, c'mon! I'm not a small guy,
but Isaac's got friends. You know what I'm saying? *Friends*.
Be easier if you all just did something about him.

MR. CHARLES

Not that simple.

DEVIN

Bull.

MR. CHARLES

No, really. You're the one I saw, so you're the one I'm
supposed to - fix.

DEVIN

Well, then what do you want me to do?

MR. CHARLES

Same thing I did.

DEVIN

It's not like back then.

MR. CHARLES

Sure it is! "Bullying" now is just more - efficient.

DEVIN

Mr. Charles! I'm trying to be real with you here.

MR. CHARLES

I'm trying to be real, too.

DEVIN

Then stop calling it bullying! He's after a lot of people; not just me. And he's dangerous, Mr. Charles; these guys don't play. You mess with them, you get hurt. So, what am I supposed to do?

MR. CHARLES

Listen to me! The two Michaels.

DEVIN

C'mon.

MR. CHARLES

Hear me out! Michael Jenkins: weenie little kid. Michael Kilmer: black hair, dark eyebrows. They were shady looking, like typical - I'm gonna break the rules here - *shitheads*. They looked like typical shitheads.

DEVIN

Please, / just let me -

MR. CHARLES

Oh, this is awful. My language is awful. I'm sorry. It's just hard to tell you about them without using the curse words.

DEVIN

I don't care.

MR. CHARLES

Well, it's against the rules. I'm not supposed to talk like that. So, these *shitheads* used to find me during recess, run at me -

like charge at me, you know? - jump in the air and kick me. So it was like a flying kick from one of them, and then a flying kick from the other one. Then they'd wind up and do it again.

DEVIN

Mr. Charles, nobody's doing any flying kicks at -

MR. CHARLES

C'mon, Devin! I mean, do what you want, but listen to me first. This is helpful.

DEVIN

Fine.

MR. CHARLES

So, twenty or thirty times every recess: flying kicks. And you'd think that a teacher would notice or something, right? But that never happened. Every recess I'd be somewhere that seemed the safest, but the two Michaels, they'd come charging over. Start flying-kicking me. I should've talked to somebody; talking to a teacher probably would've helped.

With obvious sarcasm.

DEVIN

I don't know about that.

MR. CHARLES

I just felt like a loser, you know.

DEVIN

I guess.

MR. CHARLES

And it killed me emotionally. Maybe that's obvious because
I'm in my thirties now and I'm still talking about recess in
the eighth grade. Do what you want, Devin, but I don't wish
that feeling on anybody.

DEVIN

So, how'd it end?

MR. CHARLES

I got away. Found out these two Michaels were going to the
regular high school in town, so I begged my mother to go to
this private one.

DEVIN

I can't go to a private school, c'mon.

MR. CHARLES

Oh, I know! And we can't even get you transferred out of
this one! This one's the bottom of the barrel. You apply to
any others?

DEVIN

No.

MR. CHARLES

Why not?

DEVIN

I don't know. My mom said I was too dumb.

MR. CHARLES

Well, that's - nothing we can do about that. What I'm saying
is: that private school probably saved my life; you don't have
that option. I was lucky, but you got it tough. Tougher.
Tougher than I did. So I can feel your sense of - uh -

DEVIN

Frustration?

MR. CHARLES

Seems like more than frustration, Devin. Desperation. But -
I've got a trick that can save you. A *mental* trick.

DEVIN

I'm just fine mentally, Mr. Charles.

MR. CHARLES

C'mon! I'm not saying you're not. I'm saying, I was in a
rough place, too. And this helped.

With complete, gentle sincerity.

See, I was so messed up by those guys - I just kept trying to
mentally figure out a way to hurt *them*. Like, for real.

DEVIN

Did you?

MR. CHARLES

No! Never figured out how to get away with it. But it's fun
to think about. And when I hear about guys like Isaac I start
getting that "revenge" feeling. No joke; I get like - uh -
Dexter. You know that show? Or like that Bobbitt lady? Got
back at her husband by chopping off his - you know? I just
get this feeling like I want to hurt those two.

DEVIN

Still?

MR. CHARLES

Still! I'd probably do it if I could figure out how to not get arrested. And that's messed up, right?! Now this probably isn't good advice or typical advice; I don't care. If Isaac is giving you a hard time, maybe just log it in your head - think about the revenge. It'll help, I promise. 'Cause the most I can do for you is try to get a suspension, *if* I see something; that's the rules. But you? You could put the feeling back there and just imagine - just *dream* about that one day you're gonna be able to hurt him and get away with it. Just dream about it. Now don't - don't tell anyone I said that, ok?

THE NEW CLUB

Note: In medium and large cast versions, this scene is
JUSTICE and BRIDGETT.

> *In a large hallway, BRIA is feverishly creating a*
> *large poster with a messy collection of markers*
> *and materials. ANNY rushes by.*

BRIA

I am a frickin' genius!

ANNY

Well, I'm glad somebody's having a good day.

BRIA

Where you going, girl? Get over here.

ANNY

Bria, I got shit to do.

BRIA

We *alllll* got shit to do, Anny! Now get over here and look at
how brilliantly I am getting my shit *done*!

ANNY

Fine! Fine. You are a hot-ass mess.

BRIA

Yes, I am!

ANNY

So, what is your brilliance?

BRIA

Ok, I got this paper I wrote for English, right? Failed it, but
I'm gonna fix that. It was on social justice. [medium and
large cast: cut "Failed...that."]

ANNY

What kind?

BRIA

Every kind! All the social justice! Point is, I was gonna use it
for my college essay. But it's not unique enough.

ANNY

It can be.

BRIA

Naw, Anny. Everybody talks about that stuff. I need
something totally different.

ANNY

Ok.

BRIA

And I need another extra-curricular for my application.

ANNY

Why?

BRIA

Because they're *selective,* Anny! So I'm talking to the
principal's kid -

ANNY

Andrea.

BRIA

Yes!

ANNY

That's my girl. I've known her forever.

BRIA

Ok, then you know she talks -

TOGETHER

A lot!

BRIA

Yes! And I'm like, "I don't care, girl, I don't care!" Then it hits me. Boom!

> *BRIA reveals her poster. "Apathy Club: Wednesday."*

ANNY

Apathy Club?

BRIA

First meeting tomorrow. And I need *you* there, and I need you to bring friends.

ANNY

What in the crazy-bitch hell is Apathy Club?

BRIA

"A place where we examine how *we* will never have a meaningful impact on social justice, so we should *stop caring* so much about it."

ANNY

That doesn't make any sense.

BRIA

It does! And if I get enough *people*, I start the club and *write* about it for my college essay!

ANNY

Two for one.

BRIA

'Cause it'll be *controversial*!

> *ANNY is changing the subject until she figures out how to respond.*

ANNY

Who's gonna be the advisor?

BRIA

I'm asking Mr. Charles.

ANNY

I hate that man.

BRIA

So do I, but he's perfect for this. Doesn't have to do anything, he'll just get paid to sit there.

ANNY

He took my phone today. Standing over me asking for it and I was like, "Look, let me just send this one text, ok?"

BRIA

Yes!

ANNY

What school you applying to?

BRIA

CUNY. [pronounced KYOO-nee]

ANNY

That's - ?

BRIA

City University. *Honors* College. But I gotta work it out.

ANNY

That's one thing I'll say for this school: they are on us about college.

BRIA

Yeah. Application's due by Thanksgiving. But there's like a 65 dollar fee.

ANNY

So?

BRIA

So, I don't have 65 dollars! Who do you think you're talking to? No one has money - no one *I* know has money.

ANNY

I do. How you think I look so good?

BRIA

Yeah, ok. Money's the answer to most problems.

ANNY

Facts.

BRIA

But if I get enough people to start this club, then I write about it, I can get in. I know I can. So, can you bring some people?

ANNY

Ok. Girl, ok, I'm just gonna say this and don't get all psycho
on me, but this apathy thing is offensive.

BRIA

How is it offensive?!

ANNY

Bria, this school is messed up, but kids here are accepting
mostly. You get them *not* caring, then people like me are
gonna get attacked. That's / not right!

BRIA

But Anny -

ANNY

"Intolerance cannot be tolerated!"

BRIA

You sound like a commercial.

ANNY

Good! Bria, this a safe place for me! We've *gotta* be caring
about issues here: the environment, poverty, gay awareness -

BRIA

I think we're all pretty aware of you, Anny.

ANNY

Fine! After two years, I'm fine! But these new kids I gotta
look out for.

BRIA

Kids here don't care if y'all are gay or whatever. They don't
care! Apathy!

ANNY

See, that's messed up! You *gotta* care if you want to change the world.

BRIA

I *don't* want to change the world.

ANNY

Well, it needs your help! You'd think in 2015 [fill in year] people'd be used to all kinds of other people, but no! We're not there yet.

BRIA

Anny, I could say I want to help gay people or polar bears or whatever. But you know what? That's hard work. Y'all know I'm a smart girl, but I don't trust myself with stuff that big!

ANNY

There's plenty of easy things you can do.

BRIA

Like treating people decently or recycling a piece of paper - really? If those things count, then I'm changing the world every day! And I don't get praised for that; that's just me doing what I'm supposed to do.

ANNY

Then / do more!

BRIA

And even if I wanted to change something, I don't know how! You can't just learn that. There's no "Change the World 101." I'm saying, what if I take on something important and *mess it up?!* I don't *trust* myself, so it's better to not care.

ANNY

Apathy Club.

BRIA

Yes! And so, bring some friends!

ANNY

I can't bring my friends to something like that, Bria!

BRIA

But people here shouldn't be trying to change anything!
'Cause people here'd be making it worse!

ANNY

That's offensive!

BRIA

Look around, Anny. You got Real Red Rachel fighting on the
bus, Devin freaking out on people, Isaac being a ass with his
boys. You want *them* deciding -

ANNY

You saying we're stupid? 'Cause I'm not stupid, Bria. I
might not go for "honors college," but I'm doing pretty well.

BRIA

I know, / Anny.

ANNY

And I'm doing well in spite of my shitty father, twenty hours
a week at / my job -

BRIA

I know, Anny! But some of these kids, c'mon! Even me!
Like I'd love to fix my mom's immigration issues, but do I
know how? No! So what am I gonna do, go around yelling
about it?!

ANNY

Yes! Get loud, write letters, make signs!

BRIA

C'mon, Anny! That goes *nowhere*! Stuff changes when
someone in power makes it change! Stuff doesn't change
because you make posters at school!

Pause.

ANNY

I don't think I knew your mom has immigration issues.

BRIA

Yeah, well.

ANNY

You should write about that for your essay.

BRIA

Yeah, ok! Ok, I'm gonna be like, "Y'all, my mom came here
for my education, but now I can't get financial aid 'cause I
have no social security number, she can't get a job 'cause *she*
has no social security number, and by the way, here's my
address at the top of my essay so you can come deport us."

ANNY

Got it. How you gonna pay for school then?

BRIA

Anny, Honors College gives a full ride to everybody they
accept. Social security number or not. If my essay's good,
extra-curriculars good, grades good, I know I can get in.

ANNY

Apathy Club. It's creative.

<blockquote>
BRIA

Will you come?

ANNY

You'll make an impression writing about it, that's for sure.

BRIA

It's after 3:00, Anny. I gotta go talk to Mr. Charles.

ANNY

And I gotta see Feliciano.

BRIA

Will you please come tomorrow? I need a group or it won't get approved.

ANNY

I don't think so. I'll tell some people, Bria, but I just - I couldn't bring myself to go to that. Sorry.

ANNY is reaching into her bag.

BRIA

What are you doing?

ANNY

Application fee. I'm giving you 65 dollars.

BRIA

You got 65 dollars with you?!

ANNY

Yes. And now you will.

BRIA

No, I won't. Stop it. / Anny -
</blockquote>

ANNY

Uh-uh-uh. Zip it! Zip. I'm fine. I got a job. McDonald's is hooking you up.

BRIA

Yeah, / but -

ANNY

And you deserve it. Get into that honors college or whatever; that's where you should be.

BRIA

Anny, I can figure it out -

ANNY

Yes, and you just did! I'm still not joining your crazy-bitch *club*.

BRIA

Anny -

ANNY

Stop! It's fine. Pay me back next year. Or don't! See, I care about you getting that application in. You hear me? I do care about *that*.

BRIA

Ok.

Teasing.

ANNY

You like that? You like me caring?

BRIA

I'm pretty apathetic about it actually.

ANNY

Ohhh!

And ANNY has left. BRIA has a moment to herself. It is probably a hopeful moment.

CALL HOME

Note: In medium and large cast versions, this scene remains MR. CHARLES, but all student references are changed to BRIDGETT and there is no "him-her" mistake.

> *In the school office. MR .CHARLES speaks on his cell phone.*

MR. CHARLES
Hello, may I speak with Mrs. Harden, please?

Well hello, Mrs. Harden, this is Adam Charles calling from Prospect High School. I'm Antonio's - Anny, sorry - Anny's AP English teacher and I needed to speak with you about an incident that happened today in class.

It's Adam Charles.

Yes, it is like two first names.

Like Rick James, yes.

Oh, yeah, he's great - was great - is great.

Ok, Cynthia.

I'm pretty new here, yeah. High turnover.

Well, Anny had his - her phone out and was texting during class. I noticed and asked her to put the phone away and she did not. She just placed it on her desk. I asked her again to put the phone away and she said, "I did." I said, "No you didn't, you just put it face up on your desk," and as I was saying this to her, the phone lit up with a message and she picked it up to send one back!

MR. CHARLES (CONT)

I know! This is actually the second time this week I've had to ask Anny to put her phone away, so this time I just took it right out of her hands. Anny got angry, grabbed my arm, and I pulled away and she grabbed my arm again and I pulled away, but this time *when* I pulled away I hit another student in the face with my elbow.

Oh, he'll be ok, yes. But still, an elbow to the face. And I got some bony elbows! In any case, this is what we call a "violent episode," so I'm afraid Anny will have to sign off as a witness on some paperwork -

Well, because this was a violent episode.

Yes, it was *my* elbow - but the root cause was Anny's refusal to put her phone away.

Just paperwork that'll state the facts. An Occurrence Report. It's a liability thing.

Well, why would you want to sue us?

Me, then. Why would you want to sue me?

Mrs. Harden, I think you're -

Cynthia, sorry. Cynthia, I think you're a bit missing the point. Antonio's - Anny, sorry - Anny's actions caused the -

Well, no, no not my actions. My elbow only came in contact -

I'm sorry, I don't agree with you and, frankly, neither does the DOE's policy.

MR. CHARLES (CONT)

Ok, ok. Cynthia. I didn't call to debate with you, I only called because one of the requirements in this process is that I speak to the parents of the violent student and -

No, I'm not making an assumption that Anny is violent. I am actually straight up telling you that he - she was involved in a violent episode and -

She is not a violent student. She was involved in a violent *episode*; that is my point. And so an Occurrence Report -

Yes, I should probably calm down. Thank you for the advice.

Well, I assume she's getting her phone *now*.

Uh, it's what, quarter after three? I gave the phone to our principal and Anny has to meet with him to get it back. I'm sure she's doing that now.

Oh, that's policy. We're not just *allowed* to take the phone, we are *required* to.

If it's an emergency, you call the office. There's just no phones in class. In fact, the metal detector -

Metal detector.

I'm sure it was installed to detect *weapons*, but cell phones is what it finds mostly.

They have to store them in their backpack.

They can *not* take them out at lunch. School rule.

MR. CHARLES (CONT)

It's not crazy. Used to be there was a truck outside where they had to leave the phones. Like a coat check, but for phones. *That* was crazy.

Well, would you rather have them learn to write well or take two hundred selfies? The fact is that every day we have cell phone incidents that distract from the normal course of learning -

The normal course of - it's the way learning normally happens.

Normally, yes. Without phones.

"Googling" is not generally required for AP English. And Mrs. - Cynthia, it doesn't matter what we think because she's not allowed to have the phone. It's not my rule, it is a rule given to us from above -

Not Jesus, no. Just above. Above us here at school.

Jesus could be considered above us here at school, if you want to put it that way, but that's just - when I say above us, I mean the laws that are passed by -

No, we are not putting ourselves above the laws of Jesus.

No, I do not believe I am better than Jesus. That has nothing -

Ok. Ok, well. Cynthia, I have to go. I just wanted to give you a heads up because that is what I'm required to do -

Yes, that is my number.

Yes, this is my cell.

MR. CHARLES (CONT)
Yes, *we* are allowed to use them. Keeping phones in a backpack is for students only. *They* are the ones not allowed to -

Cynthia?

DJANGO

Note: In medium cast version, this scene remains DEVIN and ANDREA. In large cast version, this scene is LEWIS and DANIELLE.

> *In another large hallway. Voices offstage.*
> *ANDREA is forcefully leading DEVIN away*
> *from the end of an altercation.*

DEVIN
Ohhh, I'm a fag, huh?! You got me whipped, Django! You got me whipped.

ANDREA
Devin, / c'mon.

DEVIN
Yo, you should be Django for Halloween! Grab that whip, baby!

ANDREA
Let's go, / Devin!

DEVIN
Master Django, taking charge!

> *They burst onstage, DEVIN with his*
> *backpack.*

ANDREA
Calm down, / that's enough!

DEVIN
How long you be in charge, Master Django?! How long you think?

ANDREA

You are so *ignorant*, Devin!

DEVIN

C'mon, Andrea.

ANDREA

Django? Really?

DEVIN

Let's go.

ANDREA

I can't even believe you.

DEVIN

Did you see him?

ANDREA

Yes, everybody's seeing both of you!

DEVIN

No, did you see him hit me?

ANDREA

I saw him / *push* you.

DEVIN

Isaac doesn't push. And second time today.

ANDREA

Everybody that bumps you gets racial slurs / thrown at them now, is that it?

DEVIN

Racial slurs?

ANDREA

Devin, this is not you!

DEVIN

You're pulling me away, but all I was doing was yelling.
What do want me to do?

ANDREA

I don't know, Devin! I can't manage myself and you at the
same time!

DEVIN

Isaac's calling me a fag with you right there. His boys right
there; I can't touch him. So I'm just yelling. What do you
want me to do?

ANDREA

He hardly said anything - you're / both acting ridiculous!

DEVIN

Yeah he did, he did. You don't get it. Why don't you / get it?

ANDREA

And *you* don't need to be saying things / that are -

DEVIN

I'm trying to handle it! Andrea, I need you on my side,
c'mon.

> *DEVIN attempts to touch her. ANDREA uses her*
> *full palm to push his face away. She is stronger*
> *than she looks.*

ANDREA

Devin! You cannot tell a [another] black person they should
be Django for Halloween.

DEVIN

It's Isaac!

ANDREA

So?

DEVIN

So, he's said a lot worse.

ANDREA

It's racist.

DEVIN

How can I be racist?! That doesn't even make sense!

ANDREA

Does to me. I don't care what Isaac's doing; I care about *my boyfriend* acting like an idiot. Do you even know who Django is?

DEVIN

Jamie Foxx. In that movie. He's a slave.

ANDREA

He's a slave, right. He's a slave. So why are you gonna tell a [another] black person he should be a slave for Halloween? It's disrespectful.

DEVIN

It's Isaac, Andrea. I didn't fight back; I can't fight back. I just called him frickin' Django and you're going off like this?!

ANDREA

He doesn't look like Jamie Foxx.

DEVIN

It was a joke!

ANDREA

You don't joke like that. That's not you! You are not acting like *you*!

DEVIN

This *is* me, Andrea! Sorry! C'mon, it's almost 3:30. Let me go to your place; your dad's not done for another hour, right?

ANDREA

You think you're getting some after this?

DEVIN

Andrea -

ANDREA

Oh, no. No, no, no, no, no, no.

DEVIN

That's not why I want to come over! You know that's not me, c'mon.

ANDREA

I don't know what's / you.

DEVIN

This stupid Django thing really gonna get in the middle of us?

ANDREA

Devin, you can't glorify that stuff! I know you're angry, I know. / But you can't.

DEVIN

It's Isaac! But that could be a good costume for anybody;
Django was a powerful dude.

ANDREA

Ok, can you just not? You don't get *power* over an entire
history by dressing up for Halloween.

DEVIN

No, but you can by making a joke. That's what I was doing.

>*DEVIN attempts to hold her or touch her again,*
>*but ANDREA isn't having it.*

ANDREA

I just - ugh. Don't talk to me. Just don't.

DEVIN

You're mad at something from like two hundred years ago.

ANDREA

No, I'm mad at *you*. I'm mad at what all this says about
you. / Get it?

DEVIN

What are you talking about?

ANDREA

Oh my god, you are so ignorant.

DEVIN

Please don't say that.

ANDREA

What, "ignorant?"

DEVIN

You sound like my mother.

ANDREA

Good, I like her.

DEVIN

'Course you do.

ANDREA

What's that supposed to mean?

DEVIN

You're not understanding me.

ANDREA

I'm not understanding you?! You are *right*! You're acting all big, getting up in people's face, talking about slavery like it's nothing. You are right, I am not understanding that.

DEVIN

I don't know why you're on this slavery thing.

ANDREA

Because you're better than that! It's rude! You want to talk about how black people *to this day* don't feel safe in some parts of the south?

DEVIN

I don't feel safe in some parts of Brooklyn! What does that have to do with it?

ANDREA

There's a difference, Devin!

DEVIN

Why is this *your* issue all of a sudden?

ANDREA

It's *our* issue.

DEVIN

No, it's not. It's just yours.

ANDREA

People are enslaved today and my boyfriend is mocking it.

DEVIN

People are not "enslaved today" and maybe your boyfriend was just trying to diffuse a situation.

ANDREA

Human trafficking, child soldiers, labor camps -

DEVIN

Ok, Wikipedia.

ANDREA

You're not gonna tell a Jewish person to dress up like they're in some camp.

DEVIN

Of course I wouldn't.

ANDREA

How's slavery any different?

DEVIN

Again, it's Isaac, so -

ANDREA

I can't even believe we are having this conversation.

DEVIN

Neither can I. Let's stop.

ANDREA

You're turning into a punk.

Sincere.

DEVIN

I'm not trying to. You didn't like my one comment. To me, it's no big deal, but I'm sorry. You're offended by it? I'm sorry. If Isaac hadn't started -

ANDREA

I don't care what Isaac started! This is about you! This is about us!

DEVIN

I know! Ok, I know it's about us. Now. But it didn't start that way; I didn't intend it to be that way.

ANDREA

You've gotta think before you speak, / Devin.

DEVIN

Ok! Seriously, I'm sorry. I don't think about things the way you do. It's - this kid just gets in my head -

ANDREA

You've gotta learn to -

DEVIN

I know! God, Andrea, I know I am not perfect like you. But c'mon, I'm telling you it's bad with this guy and me and you're not listening.

ANDREA

I'm listening! I just don't like what I'm hearing, / Devin!

DEVIN

You don't like to hear I'm scared of this guy? I'm not telling
anyone else that; I'm telling you. You don't like to hear it.

ANDREA

'Cause you're making excuses for yourself!

DEVIN

Yes! Yes, I am! God, just forget it, Andrea! Forget it. Am I
coming over?

ANDREA

No, you're not coming over!

DEVIN

Let me come over. I don't want to go home.

ANDREA

You have the *nerve*!

DEVIN

Andrea -

ANDREA

No. Oh no, I can't be near you right now.

DEVIN

Why are you taking this so personal?

ANDREA grabs DEVIN's hand. But not gently.

ANDREA

Because I am personally connected to you! Because I've
shared everything with you the past three months!
Everything. But I *do not like you* right now!

DEVIN

Andrea -

ANDREA

Everything's a joke to you!

DEVIN

Nothing with me and Isaac is a joke.

ANDREA

I'm talking about us! You can never have a serious
conversation!

DEVIN

This isn't serious right now?!

ANDREA

No, it is. You're right. I can't be with you. Anymore.

DEVIN

Andrea, c'mon. I'm not trying to make you upset.

ANDREA

It's too much. I can't be attached to ignorance.

DEVIN

Please, stop saying that.

ANDREA

Why?

DEVIN

You know I can't stand it.

ANDREA

Well, *I* can't help it; ignorant's the perfect description.

A fuse has been lit in DEVIN.

DEVIN

I'm *not* ignorant. What the hell, Andrea?

DEVIN is too aggressive, too in her face.

ANDREA

Oh, oh. Woah. Ok.

DEVIN

Please don't walk away from me.

ANDREA

Oh, I've gotta be done.

DEVIN grabs her wrist. He holds on very tightly.

DEVIN

Please. Andrea, please -

ANDREA

Get off -

DEVIN

Hey - hey! Calm down! Andrea, calm down!

She pulls away violently. She has to use all her strength.

ANDREA

Get off of me! God, Devin! Oh my god, we are done. We are
so done.

She leaves.

DEVIN

Andrea. Andrea! Hey, I'm sorry, all right?!

SHARPENED PENCILS

Note: In medium and large cast versions, this scene is DARIA and MR. D.

In MR. CHARLES' classroom. He remains calmly defensive throughout; he's never mean.

BRIA
I don't need much time, Mr. Charles! I just need you to hear me out!

MR. CHARLES
You have five minutes.

BRIA
Not even gonna need that much! I just want to explain myself. See - I know it's weird, but I'm a pencil freak. I *love* super-sharpened pencils. I love the feeling of putting one in a sharpener, grinding it so it's all pointy. So it hurts my finger. I love that! Tapping it on my finger so it's like almost piercing my skin. Almost poking a little hole. You ever do that?

MR. CHARLES
No.

BRIA
Where I come from, people feel all powerful holding a knife or whatever. Not me, 'cause I'm classy. I just need a nice, sharp pencil. That's *my* weapon. That's *my* power. The pencil is mightier than the sword.

MR. CHARLES
Pen. It's "pen."

BRIA

No! Pens?! C'mon, mister, they're *dull*! There's no point to 'em! No point - that's a dumb joke.

MR. CHARLES

Yes, it / is.

BRIA

They gotta be *sharp*! Sharp pencils represent pain. 'Cause *life* is pain. You know that, Mr. Charles? Life equals pain. Sharp pencils equal life. Boom!

MR. CHARLES

You've totally lost me.

BRIA

I always write in pencil! It's my thing!

MR. CHARLES

Well, I'm sorry. Your content is decent, but -

BRIA

But what?! If my shit is good, how can you fail me?!

MR. CHARLES

Hey, hey! Watch your language in here, huh? You fail because you didn't complete the paper according to my instructions. And there weren't even a lot of instructions. Five pages on social justice. Typed or in black ink. Not in pencil, Bria. Not in pencil - I'm sorry.

BRIA

Are you though?

MR. CHARLES

What?

BRIA

Sorry?

MR. CHARLES

Kinda? Ok, truthfully no, I guess "sorry" isn't the right word. But I feel bad.

BRIA

You don't feel bad. If you did you'd just give me a grade based on what I wrote, not what I wrote it with. I should drop this class. It doesn't make any *sense*!

MR. CHARLES

It does make sense, Bria. These are the rules. This is exactly how the world works.

BRIA

It's not! The real world has *flexibility*! I'm working at McDonald's and I show up late, I'm still getting paid. I'm not "exactly" on time, but mister, I'm still getting paid.

MR. CHARLES

From the time you show up, but not for the time you / missed.

BRIA

No, you get paid for the time you were on the schedule for.

MR. CHARLES

Bria, that is not true at all.

BRIA

It is true! You're allowed a break in the real world.

MR. CHARLES

I have no idea where you get that from! It's totally, one hundred percent wrong.

                            BRIA
It's not.

                         MR. CHARLES
Bria, out in the world you might catch a break *sometimes*,
but pretty much most of the time you gotta play by the rules.
This past summer my daughter applied for her first job.
Interviewed, got an email saying she *got* the job. They said
"reply before the weekend." She replied on Saturday. They
said, "Sorry. That's a day late. No more job."

                            BRIA
That's bullshit.

                         MR. CHARLES
That's how the world works! And please, follow at least *one*
of the rules by not cursing.

                            BRIA
You follow the rules by giving me a fair grade.

                         MR. CHARLES
Well, I am following them, Bria. And I'm pretty much done
with this conversation. It must be 3:30.

                            BRIA
If I'm staying in this class, then I need a decent grade.

                         MR. CHARLES
I'm sorry - I do feel bad, but -

                            BRIA
Aren't you supposed to want to teach me? How is this
teaching me?

MR. CHARLES
I don't want to teach you that much, Bria! I seriously don't. I don't want to have conversations like this, I don't want to have to make calls home. So I make the rules very clear so it's easy for both of us to know what's expected.

BRIA
You don't want to teach me?

MR. CHARLES
Not enough to make exceptions, no.

BRIA
You're old; you're supposed to be caring about this.

MR. CHARLES
About what?

BRIA
Making a difference!

MR. CHARLES
I'm not sure one social justice paper is making / a difference.

BRIA
Aren't teachers supposed to be passionate about that kind of stuff?

MR. CHARLES
Some are.

BRIA
But not you.

MR. CHARLES
No, not me.

                    BRIA
Well maybe you should tell us that.

                    MR. CHARLES
I'm telling you right now!

                    BRIA
I knew y'all hated us.

                    MR. CHARLES
I certainly do not hate you, Bria.

                    BRIA
You're a *teacher*!

                    MR. CHARLES
Yes!

                    BRIA
You're supposed to be *honorable*.

                    MR. CHARLES
I *feel* pretty honorable! I am very, very fair. The rules are the
same for everyone. Can we please be done?

                    BRIA
I've got one possible school, mister. One chance at a full
ride.

                    MR. CHARLES
You've only failed this one paper.

                    BRIA
They look at my grades *this* semester! *This* month!

MR. CHARLES

Well, I already told you guys you could do a new one for partial credit. At least one of your classmates is already doing that.

BRIA

Partial credit.

MR. CHARLES

Yes. Five pages on the modern media. Typed or in black ink.

BRIA

Yeah, I get it. You don't care about teaching.

MR. CHARLES

I do, Bria, but c'mon! It's just a job. I work, I get paid, I go home. And I can't go home today until you leave!

BRIA

You care about the job, but you don't care about us.

MR. CHARLES

No, I just don't care about any of this philosophy you think I should have. Buddy of mine works over on Wall Street; nobody says he has to care about what he's doing. He works for his family. That's who he cares about.

BRIA

But you're supposed to be different.

MR. CHARLES

Why?! Why am I supposed to be different?! You kids are awesome sometimes, and a pain in the ass sometimes. Pardon my language. I treat everybody the same! You don't get a break, but nobody else does either.

BRIA

Teachers should be trying to make a difference. Y'all should be better than that.

MR. CHARLES

Well, we're not! Man, I hate that movie *Lean On Me*. It set the bar *so high*! I'm not here to make a difference, Bria. I'm just here to work, treat everybody equally, and go home. I work for my family, and my family's at home. So can I please go home?

BRIA

That's it then?

MR. CHARLES

Yes, that's it. Failed 'cause you didn't follow the instructions. Do the new paper if you want to.

BRIA

For partial credit.

MR. CHARLES

Yes, I'm sorry. Sort of sorry. Whatever.

BRIA

Yeah, whatever.

MR. CHARLES

Yeah. Whatever.

BORED

Note: In medium cast version, this scene remains ANNY and DEVIN. In large cast version, this scene is KIARRA and RACHEL.

> *An accidental meeting in the far reaches of another large hallway. ANNY stops DEVIN, who still clutches his backpack.*

ANNY

Ohhh look, look, *look* who we have here. Hey, stop. Look at me, look. You see this?! This is not a happy face right here.

DEVIN

Get out of my way, Anny.

ANNY

Oh, no! No, no, no - you are going to stand there, and you are going to *listen* to me.

DEVIN

Anny -

> *DEVIN tries to get around ANNY without too much confrontation, but ANNY will just not let him pass. She manages to find many ways to block the path.*

ANNY

Stop! I am serious.

DEVIN

So am I. You need to move; I gotta get Andrea [Makala].

ANNY

This is how teachers must be feeling every day.

DEVIN

What?

ANNY

Like when they're trying to educate people but not a soul
will listen!

DEVIN

What are you talking about?

ANNY

I am talking about *you*! You, Devin! In English. You could
not shut up / for one minute!

DEVIN

I didn't do anything to you.

ANNY

I actually worked on that project. A lot. And you could not -
shut - up.

DEVIN

You were on your phone the whole class!

ANNY

I'm saying when I was giving my speech. That was my time.
For my grade. And because of you, I didn't get to finish.

DEVIN

Since when do you care about your grades?

ANNY

Since always. But you just disrespected me -

DEVIN

I didn't disrespect you, Anny. C'mon, move.

ANNY

You did! You did, Devin. I got through - what? - half a
sentence? "At the beginning of Oedipus Rex, the
townspeople..." Bam! You're going off, throwing your book
on the floor or something?

DEVIN

I threw it *at* someone. Nothing to do with you. Why do you
even care? That book is so -

ANNY

I don't care what you think about the book! I need the grade.
I was up there talking, not you.

DEVIN

I got bigger things to worry about, Anny.

ANNY

Worry about them on your own time then! Not my time!

DEVIN

Anny, I'm not even taking that Regents, so the class is like
redundant.

ANNY

This is not about you - you are so dense! It was my time, and
I am a junior in your 10th grade English; clearly, I need this
more than you do!

DEVIN

"Clearly," you should've passed it the first time.

ANNY

You know how last year was for me, and you're gonna say
that? You know how it was before my father left, and you're
gonna -

DEVIN

That class doesn't matter, Anny!

ANNY

And *that's* what I hate about this school. Everyone wants respect, but nobody's willing to give it.

DEVIN

I got respect for you, Anny. Everybody here does; that's not the point. Now move. Andrea [Makala] come by here?

ANNY

She's probably home!

DEVIN

Not yet. I've been by the door.

ANNY

How many doors we got here, dumbass?

DEVIN

Get out of my way Anny or I will pick you up and throw you, I swear to god.

ANNY

See, that's not respect.

DEVIN

You want to test me today?

ANNY

I want to *confront* you, Devin. Something's going on with you, I get that. But it's not my fault.

DEVIN

I have respect for you, or else I wouldn't be talking to you right now. But it is impossible to sit in there and listen to *anyone*.

ANNY

Aw, that's real / nice.

DEVIN

There's way more important shit going on than that class, Anny.

ANNY

For all of us, yeah. But if you can't handle it, then don't come and bother those of us who need it. Or come to class and just sit there, how hard is that?

DEVIN

Hard! It's hard to sit in a room full of people on their phones, eating Cheetos, throwing shit around.

ANNY

It was *you* who threw shit around!

DEVIN

And you know we've got nothing to do in there.

ANNY

It's school. We're not here for no reason.

DEVIN

That class doesn't matter.

ANNY

To you. 'Cause you can't handle it.

DEVIN

No, it's actually demeaning. Mr. Charles just going on /
about -

ANNY

Well, what's he supposed to do? What would you do?

DEVIN

I don't know! He's the one getting paid to figure that out!

ANNY

You act so entitled, like the world owes you something.

DEVIN

All right, you want to talk about the actual class. Fine. He
had a chance! When we started, he was talking about *real*
things - building websites, putting out movie reviews and
shit. Did that happen?

ANNY

Why do you need him? Do it yourself.

DEVIN

That's not the point! He started with my respect and my
attention, but he lost it. Just like you're losing it right now.
Move.

*DEVIN finally passes ANNY. ANNY yells after
him.*

ANNY

I got my issues with that guy, too, Devin! But what would
happen if we all walked away from people just 'cause we
were bored?! That's just dumb; you are a dumb little boy
[girl]!

And DEVIN charges back. He's intense.

DEVIN

Don't *say* that again! No one can sit in these rooms all day
and not go crazy! Doesn't make me stupid.

ANNY

You got anger issues.

DEVIN

Yeah, I'm getting real angry right now, yeah.

ANNY

No, you got actual diagnosable issues. ADD or something? I
know. You go out with my best friend, so I'm gonna look out
for both of you right now. You taking something for it?

DEVIN

Anny, watch yourself.

ANNY

You take meds?

DEVIN

No!

ANNY

You go to counseling or something?

DEVIN

No, Anny -

ANNY

Ok, *that's* why you're throwing books.

DEVIN

Seriously, Anny -

ANNY

Sorry, but this whole thing about you're bored? That's not the problem! I don't want get all Dr. Phil, but you gotta control yourself!

DEVIN

Anny -

And maybe ANNY is mocking a bit.

ANNY

"Devin." ["Real Red Rachel."] You went off on the nine bus because of this, I saw you. I'm trying to talk to you straight.

DEVIN

Stop.

ANNY

We all have to cope, there's no shame. You got a mental issue? Only shame if you don't handle it.

DEVIN

I don't even know why you're -

ANNY

Because I actually like you! But I'm pissed off at you and I'm *right*.

DEVIN

I control myself fine.

ANNY

Then why couldn't you let me speak today? I am trying to give you a way to explain it. I'm trying to give you an *excuse* for why you were shitty to me because we have history. You don't want it? You're telling me you were just shitty for no reason.

DEVIN

I told you I couldn't deal with those people today -

ANNY

Still disrespectful. To *everybody*. But it gets to me, 'cause it wasn't too long ago that we were good.

DEVIN

We're good, / Anny! It's fine!

ANNY

We used to hang out! Sneak into movies -

DEVIN

Anny, get out of my / way!

ANNY

But when you act so *ignorant* -

> *DEVIN slaps or punches ANNY. It is a shock to the both of them. ANNY retreats.*

DEVIN

I just couldn't handle that class today, Anny. Why don't you get that?!

> *Apologizing.*

Anny, c'mon.

BUTTERFLIES

Note: In medium and large cast versions, this scene is MR.
NICHOLS and MAKALA.

>*In a gigantic, empty auditorium. ANDREA is*
>*slowly, with complete concentration, cutting*
>*herself with a safety pin. She cuts an area that is*
>*hidden, definitely not her arms or wrists. MR.*
>*CHARLES watches her, unsure whether to*
>*approach.*

MR. CHARLES
I hope you at *least* ran that thing under hot water.

ANDREA
Oh! Hey. I'm leaving.

MR. CHARLES
Hold on! You got some Purell or something?

ANDREA
No.

MR. CHARLES
I do. Hold on.

>*He fishes it out.*

ANDREA
Thanks.

MR. CHARLES
Better than nothing. Safety pin? I'm guessing that's not your
weapon of choice.

ANDREA

No.

MR. CHARLES

Didn't plan on this today, huh?

ANDREA

No.

MR. CHARLES

So, I didn't mean to barge in on you. But actually I'm sure
you're not supposed to be in here.

ANDREA

True.

MR. CHARLES

Quarter to four; trying to head out. I was just cutting
through.

Perhaps ANDREA notices his choice of words.

ANDREA

Ok.

MR. CHARLES

Bad day for you?

ANDREA

Boyfriend.

MR. CHARLES

Yup. Freshman?

Does he recognize her? Maybe.

ANDREA

Yeah.

MR. CHARLES

So, you're new. Me, too. Last school closed. All summer I
didn't know where I'd be, and then they were gonna put me
in Sheepshead Bay but then something happened there and
then like September 1st they said, "You're going to
Prospect." So here I am. [medium and large cast: cut to "I'm
Mr. Charles. English."]

ANDREA

You have Devin.

MR. CHARLES

Yes.

ANDREA

He has issues.

MR. CHARLES

Seems to be working through them.

ANDREA

Not really.

MR. CHARLES

I'm Mr. Charles. English.

ANDREA

Andrea.

MR. CHARLES

Andrea, who's at home?

ANDREA

No one.

MR. CHARLES

I mean like who's in your household?

ANDREA

Oh, just my dad.

MR. CHARLES

Ok, so this is the kind of thing that he should actually know about.

ANDREA

No! Please, don't tell him!

MR. CHARLES

Wait! Not me! I'm not gonna tell him. I'm just saying, if *you* do before -

ANDREA

I can't do that, Mr. Charles.

MR. CHARLES

Pretty strict rule: I'm gonna have to report this.

ANDREA

No!

MR. CHARLES

Andrea, I definitely / have to.

ANDREA

Don't report it! I hardly ever do this! I mean, it's been a *long* time!

MR. CHARLES

Good.

ANDREA

And I've tried telling my dad already!

MR. CHARLES

Oh - ok.

ANDREA

It didn't help! Telling him won't help, ok?

MR. CHARLES

Look, I'm not saying I'm an expert, but if you / let him know -

ANDREA

No! I know I shouldn't be doing this. I know! But Mr. Charles, it works, ok?

MR. CHARLES

No, that's / no good.

ANDREA

It helps! Seriously. I get angry? Stressed out? This actually makes it go away. It actually does.

MR. CHARLES

No, / Andrea -

ANDREA

You want me to drink? You want me to be a pothead?

MR. CHARLES

No, I do not want you to / be a pothead.

ANDREA

'Cause that's one way I could handle it. There's a lot of stuff I've gotta do and a lot of people I've gotta worry about and I need to deal – I gotta deal with it *somehow*! And this is how.

ANDREA (CONT)

This works. This totally works. And this really isn't the worst choice.

MR. CHARLES

Andrea -

ANDREA

It isn't the worst choice.

MR. CHARLES

Andrea, I will have to report / that I found you -

ANDREA

Please! When I told my dad, he flipped out. I didn't talk to him for like a good four months. That's not gonna help.

MR. CHARLES

Well I can't / just pretend -

ANDREA

But I'm helping *myself*! I swear. I started doing this thing - the butterfly project? It's this thing - every cut I make, I have to draw a butterfly on it. Every one. So it's like a reminder. It sounds stupid, but it helps; I'm not doing this as often as I used to. And I got a pen so I can draw the butterfly on myself right away. You don't need to / report -

MR. CHARLES

Stop! Stop, you got the rules wrong.

ANDREA

Huh?

MR. CHARLES

The rules. You got the rules wrong for the butterfly project.

ANDREA

What are you talking about?

MR. CHARLES

Well, I don't want to dismiss you trying to help yourself, but you're - doing it wrong.

ANDREA

It's helping, I'm not -

MR. CHARLES

You said you draw a butterfly on top of a cut.

ANDREA

Well, not like all over it. Not like on the - the scab, / and -

MR. CHARLES

Yeah, ok - not all over it. But you said every cut you make, you have to draw a butterfly on it. That's not the rules.

ANDREA

Well, what are your rules then?

MR. CHARLES

They're not my rules! Not mine! They're just the rules of the butterfly project. You don't draw on the cut you already made. You draw a butterfly *instead* of cutting yourself in the first place. That's how you do it.

ANDREA

Some of us need help for cuts we already made.

MR. CHARLES

Yes! Yes, I'm sorry. I know. But maybe, I don't know, invent your own project for that. Like the caterpillar project or something.

ANDREA

Ok, you're starting to get me mad.

MR. CHARLES

No! C'mon! I just – I don't want you to misname the thing
you do. Cause you're doing your own thing! And if it helps,
that's awesome.

ANDREA

Uh-huh.

MR. CHARLES

But the butterfly project thing. You're supposed to draw on
yourself whenever you get the urge to - you know. And
you've gotta use a permanent marker. Like, a Sharpie. Get it
right in your skin. And you name the butterfly after someone
who cares about you.

ANDREA

I'm not gonna *name* something I draw on -

MR. CHARLES

Yes! You have to name it. Then no washing it off. It's gotta
fade away by itself. And if you cut your skin where the
butterfly is - you kill it. You kill it and you lose. Actually, the
rules say you kill all the butterflies. You kill them *all* if you
cut just one. That always seemed a little extreme to me
though. That rule's a little unfair.

ANDREA

Mr. Charles.

MR. CHARLES

Yeah.

ANDREA

How do you know all this?

MR. CHARLES
Urban Dictionary.

ANDREA
Seriously?

MR. CHARLES
Yeah. I looked it up. I thought it was a very good idea.

ANDREA
Why'd you look it up?

MR. CHARLES
Well - cutting. That's popular. Unfortunately.

ANDREA
Yeah.

MR. CHARLES
They say about 1% of high schoolers do it all the time.
That'd be like 20 students just in this building. It's probably
more, though.

ANDREA
Yeah, a bunch more. There's a lot.

MR. CHARLES
I know. The numbers are hard to - hard to get, you know?
Not many people talk about it so openly like you do. You're
pretty talkative.

ANDREA
Well, they *should* talk about it.

MR. CHARLES
Totally agree. But you're the exception, you know?

ANDREA

I'm weird.

MR. CHARLES

Yes, totally weird! You know, I think if you talk to your
father about it -

ANDREA

I can't talk to him like this!

MR. CHARLES

You've been talking kind of a lot to me who you just met, /
but you can't -

ANDREA

Seriously, I can't talk to him, ok?! So, what? You just read
Urban Dictionary - like for fun?

MR. CHARLES

No! No, it's - my daughter.

ANDREA

Your daughter.

MR. CHARLES

Yeah. She's thirteen. And she -

ANDREA

Ok, yeah.

MR. CHARLES

So, I looked it up. Gave her this idea 'cause I couldn't find
any other way to - help.

ANDREA

So that's nice.

MR. CHARLES
Yeah, well. So I get it. I get what you're doing. I mean, I won't pretend to be in your shoes or whatever, but - I get what you're doing.

ANDREA
Yeah, thanks.

They are connected. Playful.

MR. CHARLES
Even though you're doing it wrong.

ANDREA
Hey!

MR. CHARLES
It's true!

ANDREA
You're ridiculous.

MR. CHARLES
I totally know that already.

ANDREA
What are the rules again?

MR. CHARLES
Draw the butterfly - permanent marker - *instead* of cutting. Not after.

ANDREA
Yeah.

MR. CHARLES
And name it. After someone who cares about you.

ANDREA
I can try that.

MR. CHARLES
Yeah! Just try it. That's all I'm saying. Try the real rules.
And tell your father.

ANDREA
Mr. Charles -

MR. CHARLES
Tell him. Try it again. Just try.

ANDREA
He doesn't want to hear / about -

MR. CHARLES
I swear he wants to help. Probably has no idea how to, but I
know he wants to.

ANDREA
Ok! God!

MR. CHARLES
Ok!

ANDREA
Can you just not report it?

MR. CHARLES
No, no I have to report it.

ANDREA
But if / he hears -

MR. CHARLES

Wait. I can wait a couple days. That's not really - I mean, it's breaking the rules a bit, but - then you can tell him when you're calmer.

ANDREA

Ok. Thanks.

MR. CHARLES

And take this -

ANDREA

A Sharpie. Fancy Sharpie.

MR. CHARLES

Yeah, super fancy. Stainless steel. Fancy.

ANDREA

Ok, that's awesome.

It really is.

Thanks.

ANDREA is nearly gone.

MR. CHARLES

Hey. If you want a name for your next - "Mr. Charles." Because you name them after -

ANDREA

Yeah, Mr. Charles. Maybe I will.

MR. CHARLES

Talk to your father!

ANDREA has left. MR. CHARLES remains for a moment alone. He pulls out his phone.

RESOLVED

Note: In medium and large cast versions, this scene remains DEVIN.

> *DEVIN is alone with his backpack. He lashes out in some way against the building. DEVIN texts ANDREA. He does not speak, but we see the communication projected. It is possible that we also see physical or projected images from DEVIN's day.*

DEVIN

< Messages **Andrea** Details

Where r u?

I'm sorry.

Ok?

Did u go home?

Plz can I come over? I need to talk to u

Fine

Things get better today

I know u think I'm blaming him and I'm sorry but YES I have to and u don't even know half of what he's done

He's the one getting to me. Not u. And I'm sorry I'm taking it out on u but I need u right now. Ok?

DEVIN (CONT)
It's all about him and without him YOU and I are fine

Cmon where r u?

Things will get better. Promise

Today.

EXPRESS HERSELF

Note: In medium cast version, this scene remains ANDREA and ANNY. In large cast version, this scene is JESSICA and ANNY.

> *ANDREA and ANNY at a bathroom mirror. If performing the small or medium cast version, ANDREA is helping ANNY apply cover-up over the area where she was slapped or punched. If performing the large cast version, this is the first time we see ANNY and she probably is touching up her own makeup. She is transgender and dressed in stylishly simple, feminine clothes. Her appearance is not over-the-top in any way. She is probably quite pretty.*

ANDREA

Why are we [am I] so small? Look at us [me]. Short is not cute.

ANNY

You're funny.

ANDREA

I'm not trying to be funny! I'm serious, Anny.

ANNY

Girl, nobody cares if you're short, they're only talking cause you're ugly.

ANDREA

Shut up! Get out of my bathroom!

ANNY

No! Trans girls are allowed in here, too. That's official now.

ANDREA

Well, why didn't I get a vote?!

ANNY

'Cause you ain't a principal yet!

*ANDREA pulls or touches ANNY's hair because
she knows this is a no-no.*

Don't you touch my weave, girl! Get your dirty little hands
off me!

ANDREA

It's looking a little stiff up there, Anny. Hurricane Sandy'd
come in and your shit won't feel the breeze.

ANNY

Preach! [large cast: cut to "That looks good."]

ANDREA checks her text messages.

ANDREA

Are you ok? Doesn't hurt?

ANNY

No.

ANDREA

I can't believe he hit you.

ANNY

Please. I have been hit much harder and much longer than
that. That boy was gentle.

ANDREA

He's an ass.

ANDREA puts phone down.

ANNY
I know.

ANDREA
How did I not see that? Turn.

ANDREA applies more cover-up.

ANNY
Woah, not too much! I ain't no RuPaul!

ANDREA
Sorry! Sorry.

ANNY takes over the makeup application.

ANNY
So he used to be good to you.

ANDREA
At first. But he's changing.

ANNY
He's got serious issues, girl.

ANDREA
I know. But - I *liked* him, Anny! You know he was my first -

ANNY
I know, boo. He was looking for you.

ANDREA
Didn't find me. [small cast: add "I was in the auditorium."]

ANNY

Sorry if I was getting between you guys.

ANDREA

No, you weren't. Well, maybe your face was just now!

ANNY

Hey!

ANDREA

You sure you're ok?

ANNY

Yes! Nothing MAC can't fix.

ANDREA

That looks good.

ANNY

I know it does! I mean this foundation is like three years old and kinda nasty but yes, yes it still looks good.

ANDREA

Oh god.

ANNY

Days like this it is just good to have you around again, girl. Finally. You made me do two years here without you.

ANDREA

You're the best thing about this place. Where are you going now?

ANNY

Doing some quick shopping, then home. What is it, 4:00?

ANDREA

You want to buy me a slice first?

ANNY

No, I do not want to buy you pizza, bitch! You buy your own damn slice.

ANDREA

I don't even have a dollar! Come on, I don't want to go home. Fix my hair?

ANNY

Ok, but quick.

ANDREA

No, I want it done right.

ANNY

Boo, I've still got to go out and buy some shit and then I have *got to get home*. I'll fix you up quick, but you're not getting regular treatment. You want me to put some hair in?

ANNY begins pulling hair from her bag.

ANDREA

No! I don't want your pack weaves!

ANNY

Hey - this is good shit right here! I'm sorry; God did not bless me with instant hair growth. But I can go to the 99-cent store and just be like, "*pass the weave.*"

Whipping hair out of her bag causes ANNY to drop some.

ANDREA

Uh-oh! Tumble weave!

ANNY

Shut up!

ANNY gathers the fallen hair.

ANDREA

Eww, are you keeping it?!

ANNY

This is quality 99-cent shit!

ANDREA

From a bathroom floor.

ANNY

Well, it's not like I'm gonna be licking it.

ANDREA

Throw it out, Anny! Gross! I'll come shopping with you. I'm not ready for my father.

ANNY

I hear that, but I gotta do this trip alone, boo.

ANDREA's phone buzzes.

ANDREA

Your mom just texted me.

ANNY grabs the phone and looks.

ANNY

That - ooo - that gets me so mad. I already promised that woman.

ANDREA

Your dad's home?

ANNY

About to be.

ANDREA

Why didn't you tell me?

ANNY

We just found out! He was supposed to be another two
months. The Army doesn't tell you anything.

ANDREA

So he's home now?

ANNY

In like an hour.

ANDREA

How long's it been since you've seen him?

ANNY

A year maybe.

ANDREA

And you still haven't told him / about - ?

ANNY

No!

ANDREA

Oh my god.

ANNY

Wasn't 'til after he left I got all Caitlyn Jenner. We weren't
gonna tell him while he was overseas; he'd be killing *extra*
people the day he finds out about this.

ANDREA

So, you're telling him now?!

ANNY

Please don't worry about it.

ANDREA looks at her phone.

ANDREA

"Anny's father home. Plz get her to change."

ANNY

My blessed mother. Always praying to Jesus that she "will
learn to accept me as I am." But now my father's home, she
wants me to be someone different.

ANDREA

Are you just gonna like walk in the door? Or do you have a
plan?

ANNY

Oh, we've *had* a plan. She just doesn't think I'm gonna do it.

ANDREA

What is it?

ANNY

I'm gonna buy something cheap and throw it on over this.

ANDREA

Wait? What?!

108

ANNY

I'm gonna get a big ol' hoodie or something.

ANDREA

But, Anny, that's not you! You should be telling him!

ANNY

Oh, don't even. You are *not* one to talk about father-daughter communication.

ANDREA

Touche'.

ANNY

Honey, I do what I need to do. I know I'm beautiful, that's what matters.

ANDREA

I know you are, too. But -

ANNY

No but! Just beauty.

>*Sing-songy.*

"No butt, just beauty. Heyyy!"

ANDREA

Everybody thinks you're beautiful, Anny. He will, too, if you show him.

ANNY

Not yet. Just not yet.

ANDREA

Anny -

ANNY

After he called last night, my mom asked if you'd play my girlfriend again.

ANDREA

Ok, that *was* fun.

ANNY

No! Eww! / God!

ANDREA

Eww?! You bitch! Anny, you're past all that, c'mon. I'm surprised at you right now.

ANNY

No need to be surprised, girl. Just trying to survive. That's one thing I am fabulously good at: surviving. So, I'll change and lay this beauty on him later.

ANDREA

That's ridiculous. It's ridiculous, you're like one of the most popular people here. Especially this year! You're an inspiration. But giving in 'cause your father's back from - ?

ANNY

Afghanistan.

ANDREA

So you deny who you are because - you're afraid of him?

ANNY

I denied who I am since I was eight! I don't think one more day will make a difference.

ANDREA

You're scared.

ANNY

I'm scared! Fine! What's wrong with that?!

ANDREA

Anny. Your dad's just gonna need time to process this.

ANNY

You know how he is! I've been hit once today [enough already], I do *not* need that again.

ANDREA

This isn't the Anny I know.

ANNY

It's the *Antonio* you used to know. The *survivor*. Let me be straight with you: I can be like this in here 'cause you all *let* me. And thank God for that! But out there - people don't know how hard it is.

ANDREA

But you're so confident.

ANNY

You know me better than that.

ANDREA

You're strong, though! You haven't talked since you came out to him, but since then you've actually figured some shit out! You know who you are now! He's mad and he's violent, but that doesn't mean you have to give in and show him a normal you.

ANNY

Normal?

ANDREA

You know what I -

ANNY

You did not just say that.

ANDREA

A *fake* you! You don't have to show him a *fake* you. I love
you, Anny. You're like my hero. I'm trying to look out for
you.

ANNY

Honey - I know. You a good little bitch. You are a diva in a
tiny little smurf package and you'll change the world
someday. I'm just trying to survive the world, you're
actually gonna change it.

ANDREA is determined now. And quick.

ANDREA

Let me come with you. Don't change; let me come with you
and we'll show him together.

ANNY

Andrea -

ANDREA

Don't change these clothes! Or this hair! I'm saying, *this* is
you now! When you started coming to school like this, what
happened?

ANNY

Here was fine.

ANDREA

Exactly.

ANNY

People here got more important shit to worry about than how good I look.

ANDREA

I know!

ANNY

But it's out there, Andrea! Just getting to school is dangerous. It's like a minefield.

ANDREA

For me, / too -

ANNY

You think regular street harassment's bad; you try walking by guys on our block looking this fierce when they know who you used to be.

ANDREA

Guys in front of that bodega [store] threaten *all* of us.

ANNY

All of us girls, yes, yes they do. But after they realize it's *me* they just hit on - c'mon. They're scary.

ANDREA

They're just jealous 'cause you look better than -

TOGETHER

their girlfriends!

ANNY

Damn right! I do!

ANDREA

I know walking to school's tough. But it's gotten easier.

ANNY

Not really.

ANDREA

Yes, it has! When you're with me.

ANNY

Fine.

ANDREA

So, it will get *easier* with him, too!

ANNY

My dad will *freak out*, boo.

ANDREA

Yes. And then -

ANNY

And then he will freak out some more.

ANDREA

Yes. And then -

ANNY

He'll hit me, I'll hit him back, you'll bail me out of jail.

ANDREA

He'll be *scared*! He has memories of his *son* and you're gonna mess with that. But maybe he gets used to you.

ANNY

Yeah. Maybe he gets used to me.

ANDREA

Screw your mom. You don't have to change.

ANNY

Maybe.

ANDREA

And I'll come. I can be your good luck charm.

ANNY

This girl doesn't need luck. This girl needs to express
herself.

ANDREA

Yes! So -

ANNY

So, it's gonna be real messy.

ANDREA

Yes.

ANNY

It's gonna be real, real loud.

ANDREA

Yes.

ANNY

And you're *sure* you're up for this?

ANDREA

Yes, Anny! I love you and I am coming with you.

ANNY is nervous. This still isn't easy.

ANNY

Ok. Ok little smurf diva, you're making changes already!
Text her back. Tell her *Anny's* on her way home now.

ANDREA

With me right behind.

ANNY

Beside. With you right beside.

They exit together. Beside each other.

EMERGENCIES

Note: In medium cast version, this scene is BRIA and
DEVIN, with MR. NICHOLS. In large cast version, this
scene is MILAN and DEVIN, with MR. NICHOLS.

> *In a secluded back corner of the school, in or
> near a stairwell. BRIA is amidst a sloppy pile of
> loose-leaf and "NY Post" papers. She takes
> notes with a pencil as she reads on her phone.*

BRIA
Devin!

DEVIN
What are you doing way back here?

BRIA
You don't even know - I have had a *day*! Yo, where've *you*
been?

DEVIN
I've been around.

BRIA
No, you haven't. Been with that girl who can't shut up.

DEVIN
Who?

BRIA
Who?! Feliciano's kid.

> *He's probably defensive.*

DEVIN
What about her?

BRIA

Nothing - she's all right.

He's probably agitated.

DEVIN

You know where she is?!

BRIA

No. Yo, calm down. Seriously, where've you been?

DEVIN

Just home a lot.

BRIA

Your mom know that?

DEVIN

Don't.

BRIA

Just looking out for you, cousin, / just like - [large cast: replace "cousin" with "my friend."]

DEVIN

Well don't.

.

BRIA

Like I always have.

DEVIN

Oh, you always have, / huh?

BRIA

That's what friends are / for.

DEVIN
Seems to me it's the other way around.

BRIA
Nah, it's teamwork, baby teamwork!

Even more agitated.

DEVIN
Bria -

BRIA
Relax! I'm messing with you.

DEVIN
Yeah. What's all this?

BRIA
Frickin' make-up paper! Five pages on the modern media.
Like I don't have enough to do already.

DEVIN
You're doing it here?

BRIA
Better than home.

DEVIN
Yeah.

BRIA
Yeah, and I got this. It's gonna be something like how media
people *don't know what they're talking about!*

DEVIN
Yeah.

BRIA

They straight up miss the point! Like this girl got stabbed at school up in Connecticut, right? And there's all these stories about how the guy that did it was pissed off she turned him down for prom last year. No *way*! I'm sorry, no guy cares that much about frickin' prom.

DEVIN

Probably had another reason, yeah.

BRIA

Probably *lots* of reasons! That's what I'm saying!

DEVIN

They don't write that.

BRIA

You hear about this thing in Bryant Park? The skating rink? Same thing. There's like ten stories today on how this kid shot somebody over a jacket. No! Not possible.

DEVIN

When was this?

BRIA

Last night! This kid tries to take some guy's Biggie. Guy says, "Hell no, you ain't taking my jacket." Kid shoots him.

DEVIN

How old's the kid?

BRIA

Sixteen.

DEVIN

He get away?

BRIA

Skated away! Twirling around, nobody grabbed him or anything.

DEVIN

Wow.

BRIA

Skating off like, "Don't mind me. I just shot some dude in front of mad people!"

DEVIN

He was calm.

BRIA

Calm?! No, dumb! I'm telling you, this guy is so dumb. Police go there this morning and he's on Twitter. "Not going out like this." "Should I shoot myself?" Live tweeting while the police are at his door! This punk is so *dumb*!

DEVIN

Shot him and got away though.

BRIA

And went straight home where they could find him! Why would you do that?!

DEVIN

Yeah.

BRIA

So every one of these stories says the kid just wanted the jacket. *They don't know what they're talking about!* You're gonna shoot somebody for a jacket, right? I mean, you shoot them, that jacket's gonna get *messed up*! It's gonna have mad holes in it!

                          DEVIN
You're right about that.

                          BRIA
"Yo, let me get that jacket." Boom, boom, boom. Bloody
holes right through it. You're not gonna *wear* that shit! I'm
sorry, this was not about a jacket.

                          DEVIN
Revenge.

                          BRIA
Maybe. That's my point! When shit goes down, there's a lot
of reasons. So why are they telling us it's *prom*, or it's the
jacket? That's my media paper right here.

                          DEVIN
People around him. Influence.

                          BRIA
Now you're doing it, too - giving just one reason. But it's
more! Shoot, I hang out with punks like that. People say,
"You are who your friends are," I'm all, "Lies-dot-com."
You follow who you want to follow.

                          DEVIN
People push you, though.

                          BRIA
Push back! I've never once done anything bad! Some of my
friends have records; I'm like, "Y'all gonna grow up, you
can't get *jobs* 'cause of that."

                          DEVIN
Who cares about jobs?

BRIA

What are you talking about who cares about jobs? Yo, I got plans. City College; it's happening.

DEVIN

Not for me. I'm done.

BRIA

You're done. Yeah, ok. You're done.

DEVIN

Check it.

DEVIN unzips his backpack. There is a gun in there, and this moment should be the first indication of that fact. The gun never leaves the backpack, and is perhaps never even visible to the audience.

BRIA

What are you - woah! Is that - ? What are you doing with that? Devin -

BRIA tries to pull the bag away.

DEVIN

Nope. Uh-uh.

BRIA

You stupid?

DEVIN

No, / I'm not.

BRIA

What's your problem?

DEVIN

Same as always. Just ready to take care of it now.

BRIA

Take care of what?

DEVIN

Isaac.

BRIA

Isaac?! What do you think that's gonna -

Finally, the rage.

DEVIN

I'm done with him! Done!

BRIA

But you're not gonna - ?

BRIA reaches for the bag again.

DEVIN

No! More than a year this kid's been on me! Frickin' killing
me, Bria! *Killing* me! If I have to take it from him one more
time - forget it! I'm done. You *know* the shit he's giving me.
Everybody does.

BRIA

Relax! Jesus, relax.

DEVIN

No! I'm fine. I'm good now.

BRIA

Devin, you know I hate Isaac, too. / But -

DEVIN

Today, he's on me with my girl right there. Can't do shit back, or ten of his friends get on me. How am I supposed to take that?

BRIA

Where did you - how did you get that in here?

DEVIN

School safety's a joke.

BRIA

You took it through security?!

DEVIN

Yeah, scanned. I got my phone back here, and that they look at. But this? Slides right through the x-ray. They're distracted.

BRIA

There's like five of them down there!

DEVIN

And only one on the x-ray. Barely looking. Easy.

BRIA

So. You're gonna -

DEVIN

Take him out. Today. Done.

BRIA

Devin. I don't - Where did you even get that?

DEVIN

It's my mom's.

BRIA

Your mom's?! Doesn't she lock it up?

DEVIN

Of course she does. She gave me the code to the lockbox. For emergencies.

BRIA

This ain't [isn't] that kind of emergency.

DEVIN

You're right. This is revenge.

BRIA

You're gonna get yourself arrested, easy. Arrested and sent away. Or killed, Devin. You could -

DEVIN

I'm not the one getting killed! I'm taking care of Isaac, and doing it safe. No one'll know.

BRIA

No one will know?! Devin! What, were you gonna follow him home?

DEVIN

Nah, he stays after. "Academic intervention." Gets out in like ten minutes.

BRIA

Devin.

DEVIN

He goes out this way every day. And nobody can hear anything back here. Easy exit.

BRIA

There's no way you would get -

DEVIN

Yeah, I would. Guy's gotta pay. Simple as that.

BRIA

But the cameras -

DEVIN

You see any cameras?! No money to get us books, you think they got money for cameras?

BRIA

Isaac - he's seriously like in a gang or something.

DEVIN

I know.

BRIA

He's got friends.

DEVIN

I'm not dumb; nobody's gonna know but you.

BRIA

Son, everybody's gonna know! Everybody knows he's on you!

DEVIN

Yes! Everybody knows! And I'm sick of it!

BRIA

I get that! I get that. But, Devin. Jesus, Devin. Don't be stupid.

DEVIN

Stop saying / that!

BRIA

Ok! C'mon, relax.

DEVIN

I need to do something, Bria!

BRIA

Yeah, but maybe - I don't know. Maybe it's something else?
Maybe he deserves something else? Like this is too much.

DEVIN

It's not too much.

BRIA

It's definitely / too much!

DEVIN

Bria, stop!

BRIA

Ok! Ok, don't freak out. Relax. I just mean, there's other
options.

DEVIN

What else am I gonna do?!

BRIA

Anything, Devin.

DEVIN

I need to *do* something!

BRIA

Well, let's do it! I'll help. But not this, Devin. This is gonna
get you killed! I'm not letting that happen.

DEVIN

I don't even care. / Really.

BRIA

I care!

DEVIN

I don't! So -

BRIA

So, let's - get creative.

DEVIN

What do mean?

BRIA

We find another option.

DEVIN

Bria, / I don't want -

BRIA

Something better! To get him back.

DEVIN

I'm getting him / back –

BRIA

Not like this! We can't do it / like this.

DEVIN

I don't want your help!

BRIA

You're getting it! I'm helping; I owe you. I'm helping you.
[large cast: cut "I owe you."]

DEVIN

Bria, you got college. You get caught up in this -

BRIA

Devin, I get it, ok?! What you want to do, I get it; believe
me. But not like that. C'mon, that gun is too much. You've
been there for me, I'm there for you. / Let's just –

> *BRIA has been moving closer to try to take the
> backpack again, but DEVIN breaks away.*

DEVIN

I've gotta do this! I'm gonna / do this!

BRIA

Fine! Fine, let's just get some crazy ass revenge, ok?!

> *This might be a way out for him. He probably
> wants a way out. And she is smart enough to
> know that.*

> *We see MR. CHARLES finally getting ready to
> go home. He pauses with cell phone in hand.*

DEVIN

Like what?

BRIA

Like I don't know yet. There's more people that hate him,
right?

DEVIN

Yeah.

                        BRIA
So we go get them. Right now. We get them.

                        DEVIN
And.

                        BRIA
And we jump Isaac right here.

                        DEVIN
Yeah.

                        BRIA
We do - I don't know.

                        DEVIN
What?

                        BRIA
We do *crazy* shit to him.

                        DEVIN
Like?

                        BRIA
Like, we grab him, hold him. Hold him under the stairs. And
- like throw glue on him and shit.

                        DEVIN
You in kindergarten?

                        BRIA
C'mon.

                        DEVIN
Glue?

BRIA

Yeah, like Elmer's glue all on him. And we tie him down - to that furnace thing. Leave him there.

DEVIN

I like that. I can get into the janitor's room. I don't know about rope, but they got duct tape.

BRIA

Good.

DEVIN

But leaving him there's not enough.

BRIA

Not enough what?

DEVIN

Not enough! Not enough pain! Not enough getting back at him! Not / enough hurt -

BRIA

Ok! Ok, so - I don't know.

DEVIN

His nails.

BRIA

Yeah.

DEVIN

We twist his nails off.

BRIA

God.

DEVIN

Tape him down. Twist his nails off with a pair of pliers.

BRIA

Ok.

DEVIN

Pull them off slow.

BRIA

Ok.

DEVIN

And stick them in his mouth.

BRIA

That's disgusting.

DEVIN

I don't care.

BRIA

You really want to stick a ripped-off fingernail in his mouth?

DEVIN

Yeah. Tape his mouth closed - watch him swallow it.

BRIA

Devin, oh my god, what is wrong / with you?

DEVIN

What?! What?

BRIA

Nothing, it's fine.

                    DEVIN
And I'll take a hammer to his feet.

                    BRIA
You're serious.

                    DEVIN
Pound on his toes until we break each one up in little pieces.
So the bones are like all busted up.

                 MR. CHARLES
Leah. Hey. It's Dad. Listen, I'm heading home in a few, but I
just wanted to call. I know what I want to say is gonna sound
cheesy, but I don't care and - ok you are beeping and I am
cut off and I hate when your phone does that.

                    BRIA
Devin -

                    DEVIN
What?!

                    BRIA
Devin, I don't -

                    DEVIN
Fine! Leave.

                    BRIA
No! I just -

                    DEVIN
Leave.

                    BRIA
I can get school safety -

DEVIN

Oh, you *want* me dead, then. / Ok -

BRIA

No, Devin! Fine. It's fine. Go get the stuff.

DEVIN

Ok. Box cutter in there; I can bring that, too.

BRIA

No.

DEVIN

We can slice him up.

BRIA

With a box cutter?! No! / That's -

DEVIN

We torture him, leave him all taped up back here, and take off.

BRIA

Ok -

DEVIN

Ok.

A tortured pause.

BRIA

I'm gonna do it with you.

DEVIN

Yeah. So let's go round up some people!

BRIA

Wait.

DEVIN

What?

BRIA

I can make sure he comes back here alone. While you wait.

DEVIN

Just us?

BRIA

I ask him to come back here with me, he will. Trust me.

DEVIN

Easier with a group, though.

BRIA

But keeping it just us -

DEVIN

Simpler. Yeah, I see that.

BRIA

Give me time alone to get him - distracted. You cover your face.

DEVIN

Then I jump him.

BRIA

And you gotta tape up his mouth and his *eyes*.

DEVIN

Naw, I want him to see / what's coming.

BRIA

Tape over his eyes! I'll take off running when you come in, but if he can't see - then I come back.

DEVIN

You don't have to -

BRIA

I'm staying beside you for this. I'll be lookout.

DEVIN

Ok, good.

BRIA

But you're not doing more than what we said. No gun.

DEVIN

I know!

BRIA

All right. We good?

DEVIN

Good.

MR. CHARLES

Leah, Dad again. Sorry about that. So, I was apologizing in advance for my cheesiness.

BRIA

You gotta ditch the gun now.

DEVIN

I will!

MR. CHARLES
But I am a cheesy father. And you are stuck with me.
Anyway, I wanted to call just to tell you that I - uh - I
appreciate our friendship.

DEVIN
You sure you want to do this with me?

BRIA
I'll be fine. I'm in.

MR. CHARLES
That didn't sound right. I appreciate that we tell each other
things, you know?

BRIA
Devin - you good now?

DEVIN
I'm real good. Bria. This is better.

BRIA checks in with herself just to make sure.

MR. CHARLES
I appreciate that you actually look to me for help sometimes,
Leah.

BRIA
It is better.

DEVIN
Yeah.

BRIA
Get rid of the gun now.

DEVIN

I will!

BRIA

Well, then let's do it.

DEVIN

I'll be ready in two minutes!

They both exit. DEVIN moves first, BRIA follows.

MR. CHARLES

And I want you to know that I really just think you're a terrific person, and I'm not just saying that 'cause you're my daughter. I just really mean it and I really value how we can talk about things. And I want to keep it that way. 'Cause you and I are gonna need to rely on each other sometimes, you know? I need you, you need me; both ways, right? That cheesy enough for ya? I love you, butterfly. I'm heading out the back way - I'll see you at home.

And perhaps we see the initial text again: "Inspired by actual events." This reminder may serve to legitimize the debate that follows.

EPILOGUE

> *We see news anchors again. Character assignments following each line are suggestions only, and may be adjusted.*

A near tragedy today at Prospect High School where two teenagers are being held after an assault with a deadly / weapon. (ANDREA)

A life may have been saved today due to a teacher's surprise discovery. (MR. CHARLES)

A search of the area revealed a discarded handgun, though the gun was apparently *not* used in the attack. (BRIA)

> *We see a panel of news commentators. They speak rather quickly.*

This is News Talk and we're discussing today's violence in Brooklyn. No guns used, but torture - c'mon - that seems bad enough / to me. (DEVIN)

Things at Prospect went out of control! (ANDREA)

Well, they *escalated*, but out / of control? (MR. CHARLES)

We need to get these guns off / the street! (ANDREA)

They didn't use a gun! This wasn't Columbine, or Sandy Hook. (MR. CHARLES)

Thank God. (ANNY)

It's an awful ending, but it's not even a very dramatic one. No shooting spree, / no evacuation. (MR. CHARLES)

Slicing him up with a box cutter isn't dramatic enough for you?! (ANNY)

They're mentally ill, / clearly. (ANDREA)

Look, I don't want to sound like I don't care, but this could have been / so much worse. (BRIA)

The victim is a *known* gang member. We may not *like* the way they handled him, but they handled him. Maybe that's actually a good thing. (MR. CHARLES)

A good thing?! (ANDREA)

Right, they can't always rely on their teachers, their / parents. (BRIA)

And handling things *alone* doesn't work; they have to rely - (ANNY)

> *Two voices respond with the next line together.*

on each other! (ANNY & BRIA)

Yes. (BRIA)

What, to help torture / people?! (DEVIN)

I don't understand these / kids! (ANDREA)

Of course you don't! / Who does?! (MR. CHARLES)

Saying you understand this would be a little messed up. (ANNY)

These neighborhoods are not what they used / to be! (ANDREA)

I'm sure good things happen at Prospect, but *now* it'll be remembered / just for this. (BRIA)

We report the news - (DEVIN)

> *Two voices respond together.*
Bad news! (MR. CHARLES & BRIA)

We report only the / *bad* news. (MR. CHARLES)

We're not going to report "Flight 72 has landed *safely*!" (BRIA)

No one wants that kind of news. (ANNY)

Spike Lee says / gentrification - (ANDREA)

Spike Lee?! (DEVIN)

Over-gentrification is "destroying neighborhood identity." I say not *enough* gentrification is leaving neighborhoods to rot! (ANDREA)

The act was violent, but does that make these kids / violent? (MR. CHARLES)

No, these two were pushed to a breaking point. (BRIA)

Give me your tired, your poor, your huddled / masses yearning to breathe free! (ANDREA)

Every week we sit here and talk about some awful thing some kid did and we say "how unbelievable." When do we say, "why?" (BRIA)

We do say, "why!" But the answer's always, "schools are out of control" or "these kids have a rough life." That is a ridiculous over-simplification. (MR. CHARLES)

What ever happened to - (ANDREA)

> *Two voices respond together.*
> **the American Dream?!** (ANDREA & BRIA)

Right?! (BRIA)

So how do we help? What do / we do? (ANNY)

If I knew that I could change the world! (BRIA)

It's not policy change. You want to help? Get to the motivation. (MR. CHARLES)

Understand where they're coming / from - (DEVIN)

Who they are, what they're worrying / about - (MR. CHARLES)

We can't explain what happened today, because it's messy. But you want a first step? Start learning who these kids are. (DEVIN)

Is that your attempt at an inspirational ending? (ANNY)

No, c'mon! This can't have a good ending. But it *can* have an ending that looks for what to do next. And understanding - or at least, at least having a conversation where we *try* to understand - that's what to do next. (DEVIN)

> **Blackout**. *A deftly moderated discussion period is strongly encouraged following each performance.*

ALTERNATE SCENE: EXPRESS HIMSELF

Note: In medium cast version, this scene remains ANDREA and ANDY. In large cast version, this scene is JESSICA and ANDY.

> *ANDREA and ANDY at a bathroom mirror. If performing the small or medium cast version, ANDY is examining the area where he was slapped or punched. If performing the large cast version, this is the first time we see ANDY. He is transgender, dressed in a traditionally masculine way, and probably wearing a NY Mets hat.*

ANDREA
Why are we [am I] so small? Look at us [me]. Short is not cute.

ANDY
You're funny.

ANDREA
I'm not trying to be funny! I'm serious, Andy.

ANDY
Girl, nobody cares if you're short, they're only talking cause you're ugly.

ANDREA
Shut up! Get out of my bathroom!

ANDY
No! Trans guys get to choose between the two. That's official now.

ANDREA
Well, why didn't I get a vote?!

ANDY
'Cause you ain't a principal yet!

ANDREA pulls or flips ANDY's hat because she knows this is a no-no.

Get your dirty little hands off me!

ANDREA
Oh! [large cast: cut to "Days like this..."]

ANDREA checks her text messages.

Are you ok? Doesn't hurt?

ANDY
No.

ANDREA
I can't believe he hit you.

ANDY
Please. I have been hit much harder and much longer than that. That boy was gentle.

ANDREA
He's an ass.

ANDREA puts phone down.

ANDY
I know. He used to be good to you.

ANDREA
At first. But he's changing.

ANDY

He's got serious issues, girl.

ANDREA

I know. But - I *liked* him, Andy! You know he was my first -

ANDY

I know, girl. He was looking for you.

ANDREA

Didn't find me. [small cast: add "I was in the auditorium."]

ANDY

Sorry if I was getting between you guys.

ANDREA

No, you weren't. Well, maybe your face was just now!

ANDY

Hey!

ANDREA

You sure you're ok?

ANDY

Yes! A little bruising looks good on me.

ANDREA

Yeah, it does!

ANDY

Days like this it is just good to have you around again, girl.
Finally. You made me do two years here without you.

ANDREA

You're the best thing about this place. Where are you going
now?

ANDY

Doing some quick shopping, then home. What is it, 4:00?

ANDREA

You want to buy me a slice first?

ANDY

No, I do not want to buy you pizza, bitch! You buy your own damn slice.

ANDREA

I don't even have a dollar! Come on, I don't want to go home. Fix my hair?

ANDY

Ok, but quick.

ANDREA

No, I want it done right.

ANDY

Girl, I've still got to go out and buy some shit and then I have *got to get home*. I'll fix you up quick, but you're not getting regular treatment. You want me to put some hair in?

ANDY begins pulling hair from her bag.

ANDREA

No! I don't want your pack weaves!

ANDY

Hey - this is good shit right here! Other girls are paying me five dollars to put this in. But I'm just going to the 99-cent store and being like, "*pass the weave*." That's some markup right there, but you're getting it free.

Whipping hair out of her bag causes ANDY to drop some.

ANDREA

Uh-oh! Tumble weave!

ANDY

Shut up!

ANDY gathers the fallen hair.

ANDREA

Eww, are you keeping it?!

ANDY

This is quality 99-cent shit!

ANDREA

From a bathroom floor.

ANDY

You don't want it, I will sell it to one of your dirty classmates.

ANDREA

Throw it out, Andy! Gross! I'll come shopping with you. I'm not ready for my father.

ANDY

I hear that, but I gotta do this trip alone.

ANDREA's phone buzzes.

ANDREA

Your mom just texted me.

ANDY grabs the phone and looks.

148

ANDY

That - ooo - that gets me so mad. I already promised that woman.

ANDREA

Your dad's home?

ANDY

About to be.

ANDREA

Why didn't you tell me?

ANDY

We just found out! He was supposed to be another two months. The Army doesn't tell you anything.

ANDREA

So he's home now?

ANDY

In like an hour.

ANDREA

How long's it been since you've seen him?

ANDY

A year maybe.

ANDREA

And you still haven't told him / about - ?

ANDY

No!

ANDREA

Oh my god.

ANDY

Wasn't 'til after he left I got all Chaz Bono. We weren't gonna tell him while he was overseas; he'd be killing *extra* people the day he finds out about this.

ANDREA

So, you're telling him now?!

ANDY

Please don't worry about it.

ANDREA looks at her phone.

ANDREA

"Andy's father home. Plz get him to change."

ANDY

My blessed mother. Always praying to Jesus that she "will learn to accept me as I am." But now my father's home, she wants me to be someone different.

ANDREA

Are you just gonna like walk in the door? Or do you have a plan?

ANDY

Oh, we've *had* a plan. She just doesn't think I'm gonna do it.

ANDREA

What is it?

ANDY

I'm gonna buy something cheap and girlie and throw it on before I get home.

ANDREA

Wait? What?!

ANDY

Some big ol' ugly dress from Goodwill or something.

ANDREA

But, Andy, that's not you! You should be telling him!

ANDY

Oh, don't even. You are *not* one to talk about father-daughter communication.

ANDREA

Touche'.

ANDY

I do what I need to do. I know I'm a handsome dude, that's what matters.

ANDREA

Of course you are, but -

ANDY

No but! Just beauty.

Sing-songy.

"No butt, just beauty. Heyyy!"

ANDREA

Everybody loves you how you are, Andy. Your dad will, too, if you show him.

ANDY

Not yet. Just not yet.

ANDREA

Andy - I'm surprised at you right now.

ANDY

No need to be surprised, girl. Just trying to survive. That's one thing I am absolutely good at: surviving. So, I'll just change and lay this guy on him later.

ANDREA

That's ridiculous. It's ridiculous, you're like one of the most popular people here. Especially this year! You're an inspiration. But giving in 'cause your father's back from - ?

ANDY

Afghanistan.

ANDREA

So you deny who you are because - you're afraid of him?

ANDY

I denied who I am since I was eight! I don't think one more day will make a difference.

ANDREA

You're scared.

ANDY

I'm scared! Fine! What's wrong with that?!

ANDREA

Andy. Your dad's just gonna need time to process this.

ANDY

You know how he is! I've been hit once today [enough already], I do *not* need that again.

ANDREA

This isn't the Andy I know.

ANDY

It's the *Anny* you used to know. The *survivor*. Let me be
straight with you: I can be like this in here 'cause you all *let*
me. And thank God for that! But out there - people don't
know how hard it is.

ANDREA

But you're so confident.

ANDY

You know me better than that.

ANDREA

You're strong, though! You haven't talked since you came
out to him, but since then you've actually figured some shit
out! You know who you are now! He's mad and he's violent,
but that doesn't mean you have to give in and show him a
normal you.

ANDY

Normal?

ANDREA

You know what I -

ANDY

You did not just say that.

ANDREA

A *fake* you! You don't have to show him a *fake* you. I love
you, Andy. You're like my hero. I'm trying to look out for
you.

ANDY

Honey - I know. You a good little bitch. You are a diva in a tiny little smurf package and you'll change the world someday. I'm just trying to survive the world, you're actually gonna change it.

ANDREA is determined now. And quick.

ANDREA

Let me come with you. Don't change; let me come with you and we'll show him together.

ANDY

Andrea -

ANDREA

Don't change these clothes! I'm saying, *this* is you now! When you started coming to school like this, what happened?

ANDY

Here was fine.

ANDREA

Exactly.

ANDY

People here got more important shit to worry about than how good I look.

ANDREA

I know!

ANDY

But it's out there, Andrea! Just getting to school is dangerous. It's like a minefield.

ANDREA

For me, / too -

ANDY

You think street harassment's bad; you try walking by guys on our block looking like this.

ANDREA

Guys in front of that bodega [store] threaten *all* of us.

ANDY

Yeah, yeah they do. But with me, I don't know. It's like they're on edge; they're scary.

ANDREA

Yeah. But it's gotten easier lately, right?

ANDY

Not really.

ANDREA

Yes, it has! When you're with me.

ANDY

Fine.

ANDREA

So, it will get *easier* with him, too!

ANDY

My dad will *freak out*, you know that.

ANDREA

Yes. And then -

ANDY

And then he will freak out some more.

ANDREA

Yes. And then -

ANDY

He'll hit me, I'll hit him back, you'll bail me out of jail.

ANDREA

He'll be *scared*! He has memories of his *daughter* and you're gonna mess with that. But maybe he gets used to you.

ANDY

Yeah. Maybe he gets used to me.

ANDREA

Screw your mom. You don't have to change.

ANDY

Maybe.

ANDREA

And I'll come. I can be your good luck charm.

ANDY

This guy doesn't need luck. This guy needs to express himself.

ANDREA

Yes! So -

ANDY

So, it's gonna be real messy.

ANDREA

Yes.

ANDY

It's gonna be real, real loud.

ANDREA

Yes.

ANDY

And you're *sure* you're up for this?

ANDREA

Yes, Andy! I love you and I am coming with you.

ANDY is nervous. This still isn't easy.

ANDY

Ok. Ok little smurf diva, you're making changes already!
Text her back. Tell her *Andy's* on his way home now.

ANDREA

With me right behind.

ANDY

Beside. With you right beside.

They exit together. Beside each other.